THE ZEBRA REALITY

How to create unstoppable organisational
momentum and achieve
ALL your business goals

A five step programme guaranteed to help you
achieve your goals, deliver rapid performance
improvement, significant value creation and
sustainable future success for your business

Richard Cotter

ISBN Hardback 978-0-9956492-0-0
ISBN Paperback 978-0-9956492-1-7
ISBN e-book 978-0-9956492-2-4

For my extended Family

To Eleanor, Scott, Rosetta, and my two amazing grandchildren, Finlay and Alana, you gave me wings when I didn't know how to fly, never complained when I missed another family day, and laughed when I wasn't funny. Without you, there would be no story and no book.

To all of my Team 1's, the business-critical people and the global staff who supported and believed in me, no way could I have done it without you. To Sir Chris Bonington, for teaching me about the mountains, for making me, on occasion, part of his Team 1 and most of all, for teaching me the true meaning of humility.

To my mum, Judith, who gave me discipline and an incredibly grounded perspective on life. To my dad, Barrie, sadly no longer with us but who I hope can still read this; you gave me values and integrity beyond anything and you demonstrated every day, that it's never a weakness to be a genuinely nice guy. To my siblings, Bridget, Jon, and Rae, your support means the world to me.

To Irene, you are the rock of my life. You have an inner strength from which I learn and draw every day. Your balanced alternative view is always appreciated even when I don't appear to listen and I love the way your eyes smile when you look at me. Together we created a new life and I will never have sufficient words to express just how much that means to me.

And finally, to Aidan...the inspiration in my life. No matter what the world throws at me and no matter how challenging it can sometimes feel, when I look into your eyes every morning, when you smile back at me, when you walk to me for a cuddle, when you fall asleep on my shoulder, you make me the happiest man alive.

Table of Contents

I have been fortunate over so many years of combining both my climbing career with my business and motivational speaking work to come into contact with many exceptional leaders and to be able to watch at close quarters what makes them different.

I had the pleasure to both climb and work with Richard for ten years when he was the Global CEO of Berghaus and I held the role of chairman. We summited Kilimanjaro together in the autumn of 2005, and in 2009 summited Mont Blanc together via the Aiguille du Midi route. During our time together we enjoyed many days out on the hills of the Lake District walking and talking about our vision for the future and the growth of the brand.

Richard has an extraordinary ability to make the process of energising and driving an organisation feel both very inclusive and yet at the same time uncomplicated. His incessant drive to promote the vision is compelling, when he is on stage presenting to the teams around the world he delivers a simple message which engages and unites the organisation in a way that I have seen few business leaders able to do. He has a unique ability to drill into the strategy a business needs to follow and then to align the resource of the company to deliver against the goals and objectives which have been set, again he manages to keep it uncomplicated and is able to generate enormous buy-in from all parts of the organisation.

He is an exceptional leader, displaying an integrity and humility that people around him find compelling; he has a gravitas that commands respect but, at the same time, he demonstrates to everyone in the organisation just how valuable they are to him and the future.

When building high-performance expeditions, the key is always to create a blend of capabilities and attitudes. Our success on the south-west face of Everest was driven by having the right mix of climbing skills and being able to channel them for maximum effect. It is important to allow the talented people you have to express their ability and create an environment that utilises their talents and delivers the goals you set out to achieve.

Never is this more needed than in the businesses of today. The competitive pressure of global markets is driving companies to constantly explore how they generate gains in competitive advantage and in business performance. Being clear about your strategic choice and aligning resources to make it happen has been at the centre of all my climbing summits and it is clear just how vital it is in the corporate world.

In this book, Richard shares with you his philosophy and thinking on delivering high-performance companies, teams, and cultures. It strips away a lot of the 'management speak' which is so rhetoric-based and replaces it with 'real actions' that make a difference.

Having watched and worked closely with Richard, his coherent approach to improving business performance will have a significant impact on your company.

Sir Chris Bonington CBE - May 2017

I will never forget the date, the 13 November 2014. It's indelibly stamped on my mind.

I was in my office in Guildford. it was late afternoon and I was poring over numbers as ever. Sales figures, like-for-like numbers, conversion ratios, profitability by store, product margins, and web traffic; I was analysing the business to work out how we could make it better, more successful, and ultimately preparing it for the exit sale that the private equity owners had brought me in to deliver for them.

I was the CEO of the Snow & Rock Group; a £100m turnover retail group with three unique facia's: Snow&Rock, one of Europe's leading performance snow sports and outdoor gear retailers; Cycle Surgery, the UK's best, premium multi-site bike retailer; and Runners Need, the leading specialist running retailer. We had just opened our first 'new concept store' of the new business plan in Leeds. It was stunning. It was my vision, my project, and unbelievably successful from day one.

I was enjoying my first role in a private-equity backed business. This job, for me, was about making money; the personal wealth creation opportunity that I had always promised I would take up. Using all the tools and experience gained over a sparklingly successful twenty-five-year career running and making businesses successful for other people. This was my chance to benefit alongside delivering enhanced value to the shareholders.

I was still basking in the news that my partner Irene and I were going to welcome our first child into the world. We had the twenty-week scan booked for later in November, and at the age of fifty-four, I was going to become a dad for the first time. We were just about to move into our new home together in Weybridge, Surrey, preparing for the family to grow and quite honestly it was hard to see life getting much better.

I was doing what I do, taking an underperforming business, re-energising it, shaping it, adding strategy, sorting out the people, creating a performance culture, leading with vision, charisma, and authority, shaping stakeholder sentiment with my own unique brand of insight and integrity, carrying the entire workforce with me through a journey to a better land ... in short

I was a Master of the Universe...

Then I remembered I needed to make the call to the doctor's surgery to pick up the results of the X-rays I had done the previous week Just routine stuff, of course. A bit of a chest infection as winter approached; nothing to bother me too much. I was super fit, riding hundreds of kilometres a week on the bike, high-altitude climber, super-lean physique, and a great diet. I just needed to call and work out what medication would clear it up.

And then I heard the words, 'You need to make an appointment. The doctor wants to see you,' and I just knew at that moment my world was about to change forever.

The next few weeks were a whirlwind of appointments, tests, scans, blood tests, needles, machines and hospital visits culminating in a bronchoscopy which without a doubt was the worst experience of my life. There was one surreal period of three days, where I had detailed CT scans on Tuesday, met Dr Sally O'Connor, a respiratory specialist, at Kingston Hospital who confirmed the presence of a shadow in my left lung on the Wednesday and then on the Thursday, Irene and I were in the maternity unit for her twenty-week scan, to discover that we were going to have a baby boy in late April 2015. It was an unbelievable roller-coaster of emotions.

The tests and scans continued. Detailed MRIs, CTs and PET scans; the bronchoscopy was inconclusive and on 22 December, Dr O'Connor delivered the news that the specialist team had reviewed all my results and they were 99% sure that I was facing a battle against lung cancer. I had a 5cm tumour in my lower left lung, very close to the aorta, probably removable with surgery but no guarantees until the surgeon had opened me up and could see whether there was enough of a gap to get the whole tumour out.

The surgeon, Dr Carol Tan, was in the building and could see me that day. She told me about the operation I would undergo and we fixed a date to meet again. On 29 December, at St George's Hospital in Tooting, she would cut me open. I asked her to make sure the knife was sharp. She told me all the statistics and about how likely I was to die. I told her that all I wanted her to do was make sure I lived long enough to hold my new baby. We both agreed that was the perfect goal.

The surgery was successful. My level of physical fitness enabled me to get out of the hospital in just a few days. It was a few weeks to recover my strength and get over the operation and then better get back to work and finish sorting the business out. Yep, probably need a blast of chemotherapy to be on the safe side. No problem about handling that, but the business needs me right now; the visionary leader navigating the company through a challenging trading period and some difficulties with cash flow and covenants.

So I sailed through the chemo, worked virtually the whole twelve-week period of four treatment cycles, started to ride the bike again, and in early April we received an offer from a French private equity house that wanted to buy the Group.

Wow. I was about to achieve my ultimate goal, reach my personal summit, sell the business, make myself personally wealthy, deliver for the shareholders, secure the investment the company needed to grow and flourish into the future, protect the jobs of nearly 1000 workers, and complete the task that I had been brought in to do.

On 11 May at 11.00 am I had a consultation with Sanjay Popat, my oncologist. After the chemotherapy, all my latest scans were clear; I was officially in remission.

As I sat in his waiting room at Kingston Hospital, Irene was across the hospital in the labour ward being induced. The baby was already two weeks overdue. On 11 May at 5.30 pm, Aidan Barrie Cotter arrived into the world and I held my new son for the first time. Dr Tan had made good on her promise.

On 29 May, we completed the sale of the Snow & Rock Group to PAI Partners. It had been an amazing and challenging six months. In short, I was back.

I was a Master of the Universe... again

But life is never really that easy, is it? Just when you think you have it all sorted, life has a habit of biting back at you. We completed the business sale, I handed over to the new team, committed to taking some time off to fully recover from the cancer, to spend time with my new family, take some holidays, enjoy the success that I had achieved and then work out what to do next, what was the next big challenge, where could I take my skills and experience, what would the next business be to benefit from my knowledge and talent.

So mid-July 2015 sees me flying to Oslo. I am on my way out to meet the Main Board of a global conglomerate, to finalise with them becoming the global CEO of one of their divisions. $650m turnover, 5000 employees, my next big challenge. This is seriously big league stuff. It's what you work and build for all your life. This is it. Then at Oslo airport on the way back after an intense but productive two days, I suddenly don't feel so good. This is surprising to me because only a few days ago we had holidayed in Spain and Irene had said she had never seen me looking so well, so relaxed, so tanned.

By the time I got back to the house, I really wasn't well. It is hard to describe exactly but I felt I was losing the use of my left side; there was arm weakness, leg weakness, pain in my left neck-and-shoulder area, and my balance and coordination all going. The next morning I did some Google research. What could the problem be? I spoke to my oncology team and within hours I was in A+E at Kingston Hospital... more scans... and then Boom!...the doctor returns, confirms that St George's have reviewed the X-rays and says, 'You have a brain tumour.'

And once again, I just knew at that moment that my world was about to change forever.

Now this book is not about cancer. It's not about what you go through when you are diagnosed. Lots of people way more eloquent than me, have documented the mental, physical, and emotional strain of being diagnosed with cancer and then living through the treatment and I don't plan to add to their work. This is a business book. It's a book about how to make organisations better, more successful, and more rewarding for the people who run them and work in them or are their customers or clients. It's a book which distills everything I have learned over the last twenty-five years into a succinct and I hope coherent five-step process that can be translated into improved performance and results in any business, in any sector.

My reflection of handling cancer over the last twenty-four months and the challenges I still face handling it into the future, have given me a perspective on what is really important in life.

You learn that no matter what success you have achieved, what status you think you have, and no matter how much wealth you believe you want or are striving for, it is all incredibly fragile. At the press of an X-ray button, it can all get taken away. The battles that you face are no longer about sales, margins, profits, and shareholder value; they change, they challenge you in a similar way but the goals and the objectives are way different.

My reflection as a business leader and my desire to share my learning, emanate from a strong inner belief that actually there really is no such thing as a Master of the Universe. I have learned this over the last twenty-four months; that we as leaders can sometimes fall for our own self-created publicity, that we believe our own spin and PR, and that we become a parody of the charismatic visionary leader people choose to see us as.

We are given a role— sometimes we earn the right to have a role— we accept the responsibility that goes with the role; undeniably we usually enjoy the glamour, the status, and the power that accompany the role. But ultimately, it is a role; it is a job. We are not special because of our position or our power. We are not more important because of our title or the fact that we are in charge. We do not have an entitlement that others don't.

As leaders we have a responsibility to deliver or provide an environment that allows the people who work for our organisation or company the best chance to be successful; a culture within which they can express their capability, a direction and a vision that they find both compelling and inspiring, a sense of pride and ownership in what they do and what the business is trying to be, real clarity on what the organisation needs from them as individuals, and a clear sense of what good looks like.

My drive, passion, and excitement to achieve more in the future are undiminished. I am immensely proud of the success that I have achieved with every business I have run; the growth, the progress, the improvement, the achievement of goals, and objectives. I am also incredibly proud of the people who I have helped to develop and grow along the way; watching them go on to bigger, more senior roles. Knowing that in some small way I have helped to shape or develop a career is a huge source of satisfaction for me.

The characteristics and personality traits that make us successful as business leaders, as a sportsman, as high-performance athletes, and climbers, they never go. The need to go higher, faster, better, and quicker will always be there. The desire to be the best, to be successful, to win will shine like a beacon. My conclusion after my reflection over the last twenty-four months is to find a way to balance these unbelievably powerful characteristics with some personal ones, to demonstrate humility, to genuinely be interested in others, to display integrity, and stay true to values. To be more aware of your impact, to balance the *what* with the *how*, to understand that it is not about *me* but is genuinely about *us*.

So this book encompasses the lessons and the experience that I have gained over the last twenty-five years. I left school at seventeen with no formal qualifications and everything I have achieved has been through a mix of hard work, desire, belief, and commitment. It's a book which includes all the things I wish I had done differently, the lessons I have learned, the bits that worked, the stuff that I didn't know at the time and should have, lots of things that I sorted out along the way, some that I learned at the Harvard or Ashridge business schools, lessons that others taught me, and insights that I gleaned from being around people way better than me

Ultimately, it's quite a simple book because I guess my over-arching belief is that business is not really that complicated. I think sometimes we layer complexity onto something which actually doesn't need it. The five-step process that I have refined and developed throughout my career can be articulated in very simple terms: understand where you are right now, work out where you are trying to get to, what resource and capability do you need to get there, how will you as the leader influence and inspire, and find the way to create positive momentum throughout the organisation.

I hope that in some small way it helps you to become a better leader, that it helps to improve the performance of your organisation, and that it helps to create an environment that your team are genuinely inspired to be part of.

Enjoy...

Over the last thirty years, I have been fortunate in being able to deliver outstanding performance results in all parts of my life. Having been at various stages a professional sportsman, successful business leader, high-altitude climber, entrepreneur, representative-level athlete, elite performance coach, and motivational speaker, I have been lucky enough to see the key influences to delivering outstanding performance gains in so many areas and to work with some amazing people and teams.

Whenever I am engaging with businesses and their teams, either through my strategic work, the motivational speaking I do, or just plain old sitting next to someone at a business dinner, the one question that always comes up is 'What's it like to climb big mountains?' and this is invariably followed by 'And how is this similar to running a successful business?'

It's a great question and it's fun to take the time to explain how close the two actually are. In both you start out with a clear goal or ambition: to reach the top...sometimes you can see it from where you are standing and other times you need to imagine it outside of your current field of vision. But both are linked by the same inner drive...***to challenge myself to be the best I can be.***

Like all great ambitions, it stems from a real inner appraisal of where you are now and by asking yourself the following questions: Is this enough? Can I achieve more? **Where have I got to right now**? Truly successful people transition through this stage super-fast and quickly identify that no matter what they have achieved, there will always be a new summit to tackle.

So you set the goal—the next mountain, the new revenue figure—to be bigger, better, more profitable, etc. and start to build your plan. This forces you to **make the right strategic choices** and in business and climbing this is the key phase: which direction, which route, what resources, when, why, how? Any expedition leader will tell you that making the right strategic choices will ultimately define the success or failure of the climb.

And you set off, organised, with a clearly thought-through plan. Nothing can stop you getting to the top…right?

But business is like climbing; the weather changes, conditions worsen, somehow despite the planning, you get lost on the route. You realise that the resource you thought you needed were only a part of what you really need. You need to change direction, maybe drop down in height and wait for things to improve. The goal hasn't changed. The summit is still the summit, but in a **high-performance culture**, the team learn to handle the adversity, to continue to drive through the dark nights and the days when it just gets too tough. We call this the difficult middle

And through it all, it's leadership that creates the vision and the belief that you will get there. It's leadership that retains the positive sentiment from all the stakeholders. It's not just the CEO or the expedition leader but the leaders who pop up across the team at just the right time. Expedition leaders rarely make it to the top; they usually orchestrate from summit camp and leave the glory flag to their most talented individuals. It's the **leadership** that sets the tone, establishes the values and beliefs, energises the team, creates alignment and buy-in, and delivers engagement.

But in climbing, as in business, success only comes through having a complete team; a team that is **engaged, motivated, and mobilised to create momentum**, which is clearly aligned and united and committed to achieving the goal or the summit; a team that retains belief even in the dark hours, the nights where it just feels easier to sit down and not get up; a team that can go again the next day and takes pride in doing stuff right; ultimately, a team that starts at *why* and works outwards to *how* and *what*.

Get all this right and bingo, you see the sun rise over an amazing summit, you conquer that new market, double that profitability, become the biggest or the best or whatever your goal happens to be. And then like all great climbers you reflect on what you did, satisfied with your achievement until you look around the horizon and see a hundred more bigger steeper mountains to conquer!

In the climbing world, there is a quote: *'the summit never comes to you,'* that beautifully encapsulates the core of my learning about life, about being successful in whatever you set out to do, and the core of this book. As individuals, we are blessed with amazing power, capacity, and endurance; we have an infinite reservoir to draw on in order to achieve, and the only constraints are the ones we impose on ourselves.

Hold tightly the desire, the belief, and the commitment that you can go reach your summit— whatever you define it to be. It may not come to you but for sure, there is nothing in the world that can stop you getting to it.

In Step One: we explore and drill down into where the business is right now.

We face the harsh reality, look into the dark corners, challenge what people see as the norm and create a clear picture of our starting point.

So we have a business plan. There's a mission statement in reception, a few posters with buzzwords about our vision and values, once a year we tell the team how it's all going and what they need to focus on, everyone has got some objectives, and we certainly appraise them annually.

But what kind of zebra are we? It might sound like a strange question but if you showed a hundred people a picture of a zebra and asked them what it was...a hundred would say 'a zebra.' Repeat that process in your business. Ask a hundred people who work for you what kind of business you are and I bet you get a hundred different answers. I call this...

The Zebra Reality

Failure to establish clarity across your people and your organization, misalignment of valuable resource, and an absence of laser focus, will make it impossible to achieve your goals and objectives.

Ultimately, the Zebra Reality will lead to cultural misalignment, a lack of engagement, to different functions heading in different directions, to internal politics and to doubt about what WE are trying to achieve. Internally, this is a challenging place to be. Externally, it's an easy thing to see and if your clients or customers spot it, then, boy, reaching your summit will be one tough ask.

Without a really clear picture of where you are right now and consistent alignment on what to do next, you are guaranteed to sub-optimize the opportunity, fail to reach your goal, or simply be consigned to swim in an ocean of mediocrity.

Can you imagine being part of a climbing team that can't agree on the route, weren't sure which summit was the ultimate goal, focused on their own ambitions, chose not to share experiences, and held onto resources tightly so they were alright when it got tough? An expedition team who gave up when the route became too challenging and didn't really care too much whether the expedition was successful or not?

Lots of businesses get stuck in this position and if that's you, then the only way out is a full and frank appraisal of where you are right now. It is vital that you approach this with an open mind and listen to the feedback you need. The indicators can come from a number of different sources; data and people obviously help, alignment is key, and a real insight into what has stopped you being successful in the past will shine like a beacon if you give the business an opportunity to demonstrate it.

Can you really articulate what your best customers or clients think about your business? If you asked them what they would choose to change, how close do you think you would be to nailing it? And what about your people? What frustrates them, what is holding them back from being exceptional, do they believe in the vision, the purpose and the ambition, do they get the WHY as much as they get how?

This book uses a number of case studies, including British Cycling, Harley Davidson, Lego, the All Blacks, GE, the Red Arrows, Team Sky, Bonington's British ascent of the south-west face of Everest, and Mikhail Gorbachev's reforms of the USSR, to reinforce the five-step program and provide living 'real world' examples of people and organisations across sport and business who have transitioned from mediocrity to excellence, who have pursued a summit and realized their goals and ambitions, who have delivered rapid and sustainable performance improvement.

All these case studies share one common thread; each one clearly emanates from a starting point of where are we now: **what kind of zebra are we**? Sometimes it's a brutally honest and, I am sure at times, incredibly painful assessment of what the reality of the starting point is, but nonetheless it's a powerful beginning to the journey of change and development.

As humans, we seem to have an infinite capacity to live in denial. Whilst denial is a commonly used coping mechanism and one we reference later when we look at the change curve, it's deadly for leaders. Surprisingly, though, it's not uncommon to find leaders living in denial, failing to face a threatening shift in reality, a changing marketplace or changing customer expectations.

Unfortunately, many leaders ignore or deny their new reality, hoping that it will somehow disappear or that someone will come up with a magical solution. That doesn't happen. The onus is on you to lead, to define, and to initiate the change that will deliver the new world and the path to sustainable success.

Leading in turbulent or changing times requires leaders to face and deal with the reality shift required for success. Facing reality means that leaders take the time to continuously assess and orientate themselves to the fast-changing business environment. Facing reality requires leaders to remain open to new information, and be ready to adapt their strategies in support of their vision.

I challenge you at this point to reflect on how it feels to fall short or fail to reach your goal. Think back to a point in your life when the reality is that whatever you had accomplished, whatever you set out to achieve, whatever your chosen summit, you failed to reach it or you sub-optimized the opportunity.

Mine was in the early 80s; I think it was 1983. I was playing in the Cacharel World under-25 golf championship in Nimes in southern France. It was a reasonably big tournament for up-and-coming world golfers. Previous winners included Bernard Langer, Ian Woosnam, and Tim Simpson who went on to play on the US Tour. It was a prestigious event sponsored by a big French perfume company who were in at the beginning of the growth of golf on the European mainland.

It was my first step onto the world stage of big-time golf and I was feeling a combination of excited, nervous, and downright scared on the plane out to the tournament.

To say the week was underwhelming would, in hindsight, be the biggest understatement of my life. I failed to qualify for the final two rounds and spent a weekend kicking my heels waiting to fly home. I was devastated at not performing but I also used the time to face an uncomfortable truth, I just wasn't good enough to make it on Tour, and the subsequent months as I came to terms with this harsh reality are the months that shaped the rest of my career and life.

To look in the mirror and admit to yourself that where you are right now is not good enough, that you don't believe you will ever be good enough, to face changing direction from the life, of a professional sportsman, you had always dreamed of following, is a tough process to go through for a young kid. But I have always used the emotion that I can remember, to drive me on when I have faced a harsh reality or challenges. I will never know whether I should have hung in there and tried harder to make tour golf work— maybe I could have built a living— but I always draw comfort from looking at the players around me that week, seeing that I wasn't the only one who wasn't good enough, and watching those players continue to struggle for many years at the bottom echelons of the tour.

It doesn't make me right and them wrong; they pursued their dreams, their goals and some went on to amazing success. My lesson was to understand that facing reality—the uncomfortable truths, changing direction, building a new world plan - was also a route to achieving the success that I aspired and longed for. It was Henry Ford who came out with the immortal line:

'Failure is the opportunity to begin again more intelligently'

So as we begin this journey together, I repeat my challenge to you: reflect on an occasion in your life where you can recall how it felt to fall short or fail to reach your goal. Think back to a point in your life when the reality is that whatever you had accomplished, whatever you set out to achieve, whatever your chosen summit, you could have done more, seized more of the opportunity. Hold those thoughts and reflect on the fact that with more desire, belief and commitment, it would have been different.

'The art of managing and leading comes down to a simple thing: determining and facing reality about people, situations, products, and then acting decisively and quickly on that reality. Think how many times we have procrastinated, hoped it would get better. Most of the mistakes you've made have been through not being willing to face into it, straight in the mirror that reality you find, then taking action on it. That's all managing is, defining and acting. Not hoping, not waiting for the next plan. Not rethinking it. Getting on with it. Doing it. Defining and doing it.'
-Jack Welch, Former CEO General Electric

Through this process, you are going to build an amazing team around you and an amazing environment for them to operate in. You will create a new plan that drives your business on in order to deliver incredible success. So the first step of our programme is to drill into the business and where it is right now; explore the dark corners, challenge what people see as the norm, and create a clear picture of what **the Zebra Reality** really looks like.

At the age of seventeen, I left school, barely stopping to take my A levels (which incidentally I failed miserably) and set off to pursue my dream career as a professional golfer. Like most kids, I thought I was the business— the real McCoy— and there was nothing that could stop me going on to become the British equivalent of Severiano Ballesteros; full of style, panache, blazing good looks, and with a ball flight to make angels cry. Little did I know!

I started to play as a pro out of the Stratford upon Avon GC in Warwickshire, working for a venerable stalwart of the British PGA, Leslie Ball. He was old school— seriously old school— and if I am honest, we probably didn't see eye to eye on many things but he taught me one of the sagest pieces of learning I have ever received:

'Son, you write a number, you don't draw a picture'

Coming back to the club from one of my first tournaments, I started to regale him with a description of my round; the good bits, the bad bits, the bounces and I guess my message was sort of, 'I did OK, but I just had a few bits of bad luck.' He listened for a short while and then came out with his power line, *'Son, you write a number, you don't draw a picture'*

BAM!

Right there I got my first lesson in life. You can kid yourself all you want about luck and your performance but at the end of the day...the numbers never lie.

And yet how often do we try to kid ourselves in business? How often do we blinker ourselves to what the numbers are really telling us, try to package them to make it look better, find the excuses or the 'luck' comments that get us through the month end or the annual accounts and spare us the real harsh inner reflection, which the numbers should provoke? It's more comfortable, right, to tell ourselves everything will be better next time than to face up to the tough calls we need to make?

We kid ourselves that it's an OK year, that we are holding up in a tough market, that our competitors are doing worse, that next year will be better because we have a plan, etc. and yet the harsh reality is...**the numbers never lie.**

We measure ourselves against the budget and if we fall short, we find a reason why the budget was wrong. We reset a new forecast and then usually we fall short against that. Why? Because we are not addressing the root causes of underperformance and we are kidding ourselves that drawing a picture of a rosy future is enough to get us there.

> ## When it is obvious that the goals cannot be reached, don't adjust the goals, adjust the action steps
> *-Confucius*

And while we are on the subject, there is no such thing as *luck* in either business or in high-performance sport; it doesn't exist. We have probably all heard the famous quote from Gary Player the South African golfer:

'I was practising in a bunker down in Texas and this good old boy with a big hat stopped to watch. The first shot he saw me hit went in the hole. He said, "You got 50 bucks if you knock the next one in." I holed the next one. Then he says, "You got $100 if you hole the next one." In it went for three in a row. As he peeled off the bills he said, "Boy, I've never seen anyone so lucky in my life." And I shot back, "Well, the harder I practice, the luckier I get."'
-Gary Player

Gary's quote is as true today as it was in 1962. Sometimes you will enjoy some good fortune where a change in the environment in which you operate plays to you rather than to a competitor or someone else. But this isn't luck, this is an environment shift and the strong team or the business already operating at a high-performance level will always take advantage. Luck... Nah, it doesn't exist.

The Renaissance of British Cycling

Britain has basked in the reflected glory of the renaissance that cycling has gone through in this country over the last fifteen years. There has been incredible success at the Olympics, the TDF, the UCI World Championships and other high-profile race events that have demonstrated to a global audience that we can still lead the world in sport. As you might expect, a few select and high-profile people have been at the forefront of the renaissance and have taken plaudits and praise— in most cases quite rightly— and are held up as standard-bearers of the success.

In reality, though, the amazing achievements of the recent years emanate from the late 1990s when British cycling was at a low in terms of success in world events, talent, and participation. In 1996, when Chris Hoy made his international debut at the European Under-23 Championships, the man who was to become, Sir Chris Hoy, to become the most decorated British Olympian of all time, to become a future track legend, had to sign his team tracksuit out and then return it afterwards as somebody else would be needing it the following year.

The governing body was so short of money it couldn't afford to send officials to the Moscow event, leaving Hoy and his two teammates to go on their own, with their own bikes, one set of race wheels each and a few bits of spares and accessories. British Cycling felt unloved and its cyclists had little or no expectation of success or achievement. Some things round here had to change!

In 1997, a guy named Peter Keen was appointed to the newly created position of Cycle Performance Director at British Cycling. He was an ex-racer who was working as part of the coaching network for elite riders, but he had a view, that *the numbers never lie*...and even though Britain had enjoyed some success in previous events (Boardman at the Barcelona Olympics and a couple of TDF-prologue wins), his view was that British cycling had the potential to be so much better.

In 1998 at the BC annual conference, he made a presentation and articulated his vision that British cycling would become the pre-eminent global force in Olympic cycling. Given the harsh reality of the starting point, this must have sounded like the warblings of a crazy man, but Keen was convinced it was achievable.

He also enjoyed a singular benefit that has probably contributed more to the success of British cycling over the last fifteen years than any strategy, any individual, or the winning of any gold medal. In 1998, British cycling started to receive money from Lottery funding with the launch of the

Cycling World Class Performance Programme. Now you could call that *luck*, but personally, I am going to stick with a shift in environment, which Peter Keen and the team at BC were able to take advantage of.

Interestingly, when Keen is interviewed now about what he accomplished he makes a fascinating point. He says, 'For me, the greatest reward is the broad appeal of the sport now. My daughter is fifteen and went to the track in Welwyn. When I sat high in the stands out of sight - which is what I recommend any dad to do - I saw a small army of kids almost overwhelming the coaching team. That was astonishing. One of the better-kept secrets of this story is that if you look at the opening paragraph of the performance plan I submitted for funding in 1998, we said that we wanted to win medals because we think dominating the performance landscape is the best way to develop the sport. That is exactly what has happened.'

He didn't start with a plan to dominate the world. He was able to share and communicate a vision for everyone involved. Winning and domination were massively integral parts but he had a vision that extended beyond pure results. It was his desire to create a legacy; to build something that would transcend the next Olympics; 'to leave the jersey in a better place than he found it,' as the All Blacks demonstrate in Step Three. In the final step of this book, I talk about mobilising and motivating the team to create momentum and the biggest single driver of that motivation is always providing your team, your people, and your organisation with a clear understanding of 'Why'; an understanding of what the greater good is; an understanding of what their legacy will look like.

Keen's first plan included a list of about 100 athletes he wanted to fund. It was a large group but there seemed to be enough cash to go around. The Sydney Olympics, his first Olympics as BC performance director, seemed to vindicate this approach. Jason Queally stormed to gold in the 'kilo', added a silver in the sprint, and watched Yvonne McGregor and the team-pursuit boys chip in with bronzes. But Keen was not convinced. 'We had some good results but we couldn't really argue there was a system in place or that we had developed a culture, he explains. 'In fact, it wasn't until late 2001 that the penny dropped. I needed to clear out riders and coaches who weren't obsessed with winning.'

What emerged from the soul-searching and goal-setting was a leaner, meaner machine. 'When it is obvious that the goals cannot be reached, don't adjust the goals, adjust the action steps' -Confucius

Keen adjusted his action steps. Basing themselves at the Manchester Velodrome, this smaller, more elite group started to work (in Keen's words) 'smarter and deeper' than any British squad had worked before. It was not a move designed to win Keen any popularity contests but the results were spectacular. The 2004 Games in Athens brought Britain's first two-gold haul on the track since 1908, with Bradley Wiggins and Hoy claiming superb victories.

In 2003, Keen left his role at BC to be replaced by Dave Brailsford as performance director and the success continued. Brailsford is a classic 'the numbers never lie' leader. Much has been written about his style and approach to both his role at British Cycling and also at Team Sky and we look at Brailsford in detail later in the book. Everything he does emanates from a single premise: wherever we are right now, it's not good enough. We have the capacity to make it better. Marginal gains; improve a hundred things by 1%.

This Olympic breakthrough of 2004 was replicated at the World Championships and by 2007 there was little doubt about who was the world's top track cycling nation. British cyclists claimed eleven medals in Mallorca; seven gold. Spectacular became superlative a year later when the world's finest assembled in Manchester. Britain's stars scooped nine gold medals; half of the total on offer. They also set three world records. By the 2008 Olympics in Beijing, GB was already leading the world and demonstrated as such by winning fourteen medals—as many as France, Spain and the USA put together!— eight of which were gold, winning 70% of all the track finals and breaking four Olympic records; unprecedented performance stats.

The journey of British cycling continues with the Olympics in London 2012 providing what many see as the pinnacle of its performance. When the GB team captured another eight gold medals and led the medal table just weeks after Sir Bradley Wiggins had become the first British rider to win the TDF. It was an amazing summer on two wheels.

The numbers never lie...

This success has continued into the 2016 Olympics that finished last year in Rio. Team GB scooped up twelve medals in total, with six gold, four silver, and a bronze ensuring total domination of the track events and, for the first time ever, every Team GB track cyclist returned home with a medal. An amazing performance!

This incredible shift in both performance and culture all began with a small nucleus of people sitting down and agreeing amongst themselves that where they were at the time was not good enough. In professional sport, with such visible indicators of performance—either medal tables, times achieved, medals won at major championships, or victory in single events— it becomes easier to have the hard conversation about performance and about what the numbers are telling you right now.

In your business, they will tell you the same things just in a different way. You need to find a way to drill into the key indicators of your financial pack, understand what the core message is and don't hide away from it. In my experience, the starting point for the entire journey we are about to go on lies with these numbers and your ability to interpret the key messages from them.

Look back over the last trading period -one month, one quarter, one year, one business plan forecast; you decide how long— analyse the trends you can see, look at what is happening in your sector: how are your competitors performing, what does good look like in sales growth, key ratios, profitability, return on investment, new product introductions, sales per employee, return per store, production line efficiency, cost per unit, etc. Depending on your business, there are so many things to analyse. Pick your key ones and drill into them until you understand what the numbers are telling you.

What are the numbers really telling us?

Action -

- Focus on the numbers, understand what they are telling you, and never kid yourself it will just get better.

- Identify what your key performance indicators are and track their progress over a given period.
- Look at your sector and competitors to understand what good or great could look like.
- Identify the performance shift required to deliver outstanding results and performance.
- Bin the rose-coloured spectacles and be harsh with yourself and your team.

The ivory tower is a great place to read spreadsheets, drink coffee and congratulate yourself on a job well done so far, but when was the last time you headed out to talk to the frontline colleagues and do you make a strong enough impact for them to trust and provide you with honest and open feedback?

'We should never pretend to know what we don't know, we should not feel ashamed to ask and learn from people below, and we should listen carefully to the views of the cadres at the lowest levels. Be a pupil before you become a teacher; learn from the cadres before you issue orders.'
-Mao Tse-tung

So go figure out whether you have a process for finding out what you need to know. Typically, as the leader, people want to tell you what they think you want to hear, but who brings you back the real insight from customers or consumers? What did the last employee survey tell you? How is the temperature of your organisation? Do you have a forum for listening to what is getting said in the trenches? How often do the Board and first-line managers go sell in the stores or work on the production line?

If you are committed to driving significant performance improvement you have to be able to handle the uncomfortable feedback of what reality is really like. According to the Nobel Prize-winning scientist Daniel Kahneman, each day we experience approximately 20,000 moments. A moment is defined as a few seconds in which our brain records an experience. The quality of our days is determined by how our brains recognise and categorise our moments—either as positive, negative, or just neutral. Rarely do we remember neutral moments.

Over the past decade, scientists have explored the impact of positive-to-negative interaction ratios in our work and personal life. They have found that this ratio can be used to predict—with remarkable accuracy—everything from workplace performance to divorce. This work began with noted psychologist John Gottman's -from the Gottman Institute— exploration of positive-to-negative ratios in marriages. Using a 5:1 ratio, which Gottman dubbed 'the magic ratio,' he and his colleagues predicted whether 700 newlywed couples would stay together or divorce by scoring their positive and negative interactions in one fifteen-minute conversation between each husband and wife. Ten years later, the follow-up revealed that they had predicted divorce with 94% accuracy.

There is no question that the memories of our lives are recorded in terms of positive and negative experiences. We all do it every day and human nature is such that we will always err towards remembering more of the positives. When we get home and reflect on our day, it's easier to focus on the good things and blank a few of the negative experiences out. It keeps our overall mood positive, makes us happy, and allows sleep to come so much easier.

We are all human— even business leaders— but there are times when we need to step outside of our comfort zone and reverse the ratio. When Sir Steve Redgrave was winning his five Olympic gold medals, he and his coaching team discovered that his drive and motivation to be the best he could be was heightened when his positive:negative ratio transitioned to 1:12. This was his motivation to drive, train, and work harder than any other rower; his acceptance that he just wasn't good enough.

So now you need to work out what your optimal positive:negative feedback ratio is. Transitioning to 1:12 may be extreme unless you want to win gold at five consecutive Olympic Games but, for sure, you need to find a way to hear some of the uncomfortable truths from the front line.

At both of my last two businesses, I put together a staff forum group. This was a cross-functional group, self-selected by their teams, which I met with every four to six weeks with the sole purpose of providing them with a forum to talk openly with me about what the temperature of the organisation felt like at any given time. The agenda was always their agenda, although I would use the time to communicate and respond on key topics and the success of the hour spent was entirely dependent on me building an open and honest relationship with the guys who attended. Over a period of time, we built a rapport which encouraged them to come in and tell me the stuff that I needed to hear but that on a one-to-one basis nobody would have told me as I walked around the offices or stores.

At SRG, I disciplined myself to spend at least three days every week in our stores. At Berghaus, I spent a minimum twenty weeks a year in the market, and always focused on listening to customers and the people on my team who were doing it at the sharp end. I was always asking and wanting to know: how can we do it better? what's not working? how does it feel out there? what are our customers saying?

So, recognise the positive stuff going on all around the business, celebrate the wins and the successes, and embrace feedback from all your stakeholders but when you are settled back in your ivory tower, reflect on whether everything you have discovered tells you it's good enough.

What is being said around the business that I need to know?

Action -

- Make sure that you and your senior executive team spend time at the coalface.
- Get out and listen to the people at the sharp end of your business.
- Go talk to customers and clients and get a real perspective of how it feels to them.
- Set up robust feedback mechanisms so that you can clearly articulate the temperature of your organisation.

Time for some physics, and before we start, please remember that I left school at seventeen with very few qualifications and Sir Isaac Newton, I am most definitely not. However, I strongly believe that we can use the basic laws of physics and apply them to running a business. Momentum is an amazing thing, isn't it? We see it in so many areas of everyday life and yet it's probably one of the things most taken for granted.

How many times do you watch a big sporting contest and hear the commentator use the word momentum? For example, 'The team that has the momentum going into the second half is on the move and is going to take some stopping now.' We see one team miles ahead in the game and then the momentum changes, a force is applied in the other direction and gradually we watch the final result change and unfold in a way we couldn't have expected; think Liverpool in the 2005 Champions League final.

One sporting occasion I will never forget was the first morning of the Ashes Trent Bridge test match on Thursday, 6 August 2015. With the test series in the balance, England was leading 2-1 but facing a strong Australian side, I was lucky enough to witness one of the most compelling examples of momentum I have ever seen. England won the toss and elected to bowl and Stuart Broad quickly removed Chris Rogers the Australian opener. What then happened was sheer momentum as the Aussies were bowled out for sixty in eighteen overs— the least number of overs a test team has been bowled out in, with Broad taking 8-15 in nine overs. One after another, the Aussie batsmen looked like rabbits in the headlights, unable to offer any resistance to such a powerful force of momentum, unable to even comprehend what was happening, and this from a team who two tests earlier had racked up 566 in their first innings. They were a good side but powerless against the unstoppable force of momentum.

Momentum is really a physics term; at a base level, it refers to the quantity of motion that an object or entity has. A sports team that is winning games, or scoring points, has momentum. If an object, say a ball or a bike, is in motion or on the move, then it has momentum. If a business or organisation is moving in a specific direction, then it has momentum as well.

The amount of momentum that an object or entity has is dependent upon two variables: how much stuff is moving and how fast the stuff is moving. Momentum depends on the variables mass and velocity. In terms of an equation, we can think of it as Momentum = Mass • Velocity. Let's look at some more physics in a little more detail and apply the concept to our business.

Newton's **First Law of Motion:** *An object either remains at rest or continues to move at a constant velocity, unless acted upon by an external force.* This is often called the *Law of Inertia* so, in your business, once you get started with your plan, once you have got things moving, you have achieved the hardest part providing it is not impacted by an alternative force.

Newton's **Second Law of Motion:** *F=ma. The vector sum of the forces on an object is equal to the mass of that object multiplied by the acceleration vector of the object.* Momentum is produced when a force acts on a mass. The greater the mass (of the object being accelerated) the greater the amount of force needed (to accelerate the object). So in your business, by definition, the more people you have propelling the plan forward and the more consistent the direction of the force, the faster you will make progress.

Newton's **Third Law of Motion:** *When one body exerts a force on a second body, the second body simultaneously exerts a force equal in magnitude and opposite in direction on the first body i.e. equal and opposite forces.* So in your business, the more cohesive your organisation is, the more aligned your departments, functions and people are, the less opposite forces will detract from driving towards the plan you have created.

Maybe it would be easier to give you the analogy of participating in a Tug of War contest, which I guess we have all done at some point. The team that usually wins is the one which is the most cohesive, all pulling in exactly the same direction, capable of holding strain in a consistent way across the rope, with a clear plan of how they all pull together, and not the one necessarily with the biggest blokes all pulling in different directions at different times.

My idea of paradise is a straight line to a goal
-Friedrich Nietzsche

What is really key at this stage is that we get a clear picture of alignment within the business. You have three distinct sets of resource at your disposal to increase the force available: human resource, physical resource, and financial resource. The better these three are aligned, the higher the likelihood of success.

Part of the analysis that you do from the numbers and also from developing your understanding of what is happening in the business is to build a picture of how cohesive the organisation looks and feels right now. Do you have a culture where people are all aligned behind a common set of goals and objectives and is the integration between functions, markets, managers cohesive or fractured?

Have you invested the resource behind the key objectives and did everyone get what you were looking to achieve by making the investment? Could you have put more or less resource into different projects? What stopped some working and what made others successful? Was it the investment, people, attitude, planning, or a lack of alignment between departments?

Have you suffered from the resistance of opposite forces? It's important to note here that you can have this situation and also have an organisation that is genuinely trying to do its best. You just have functions and people who think they are doing the right thing but end up doing different things to the plan and inadvertently creating an opposite force. This will, for sure, lead to internal confusion—to a breakdown of cohesion, to different functions heading in different directions— and ultimately will become a driver of negative internal company politics.

In most organisations, the successful implementation of the main objectives is dependent on some form of cross-functional integration, a blending of resource to create an outcome that has greater value than the sum of its parts. What you need now is a clear picture of whether the alignment of your organisation has contributed to either building performance or detracting from performance. Without a clear picture of where you are right now and consistent alignment on what to do next, you are guaranteed to sub-optimise the opportunity, fail to reach your goal, or simply be consigned to swim in an ocean of mediocrity.

It is important to note that now is not the time to try and fix it. You need the tools from Steps 2 to 5 before we try to fix it.

How aligned is the organisation behind the plan?

Action -

- Develop a clear understanding of alignment in your organisation: is everyone pulling in the same direction?
- Make sure all the functions are aligned behind a common goal: is the effort harmonised?
- Are you sure that you have the three key resources—human, physical, financial— truly aligned behind the key initiatives?
- Have you removed the opposite forces and can you increase the mass behind the velocity?

Now I have to admit right up front, I am not a big TV watcher unless it involves sport of any and every kind. My three greatest innovations of this century have to be, in order: Sky Sports, Sky Go, and Sky +, a combination of which ensures that I never miss a goal, try, six, winning putt, or double checkout that I wanted to see. But occasionally, in the absence of a major sporting occasion and in the event of me having a little downtime, I do sometimes watch some normal TV programmes.

Which brings me to the show *Ramsey's Kitchen Nightmares*, fronted by celebrity chef Gordon Ramsey; the Channel 4 TV series that has elevated train crash TV to a new level. For those who haven't picked up on this amazing TV experience, let me give you the skinny on what happens. Gordon gets invited to a once successful but now struggling restaurant— usually family-owned and run with at least two generations involved. It always has a patriarch who still believes in their invincibility, a customer base who are deserting like rats, a team that would quite like to move the business forward, and finally a long-suffering spouse who just wants to see her husband smile again.

So the show plays out; Gordon does what Gordon does, things change, resistance is met, voices are raised, food is cooked, tears flow, and eventually progress is made.

It's reality TV, for sure, but there is a lesson in there for all of us because it's exactly that: a microcosm of reality. When I watch the programme, I am less intent on trying to decide whether to frequent one of the Ramsey newly inspired kitchens (if you can, watch the USA series, it's way more entertaining) but more intrigued by the lessons that are there to be learned.

It answers the question, 'How can I be NOT successful?' ...and that is a question that all of us running businesses should reflect on at certain times, because only by actually understanding what stops us being successful can we progress against our ambition to **be the best we can be.**

Almost without exception, the guys running the restaurants demonstrate the same 'not successful' attributes.

- **They have become delusional**, clinging tightly to false beliefs based on a distorted view of reality; usually that the food they offer is outstandingly good.

- **They procrastinate**, talking a lot about what they want to do, making lots of plans but never quite getting past first base; they just don't believe enough.

- **They are short on motivation**, even though they continually tell themselves, their family, Gordon, the cameras, and probably the guy in the barbershop just how much they want success; they just don't have enough commitment.

- **Their team is weak.** There is usually someone in the business who could move stuff forward, but the required balance of capability and desire is lacking.

- **They never finish anything they start and continually get side-tracked**, demonstrating a blissful inability to focus on the key performance drivers.

- **They fail to direct the necessary resource into the right areas**, compounding their lack of performance with a lack of investment.

If you have watched the programme you will know that inviting Gordon into your business is probably not something you should choose to do! But allow him to direct a part of this initial step one of our process and force you to dive deep into your own business; force you to look into the dark corners and form a transparent and honest view of what has influenced you to be 'not successful' to the level you aspire to.

The Renaissance of British Tennis - NOT!

To anyone watching, the events at the Flanders Expo Arena in Ghent on 29 November 2015, when Team GB won the Davis Cup for the first time since 1936, could easily be defined as the culmination of the renaissance of British tennis in much the same way as I have described the development of cycling over the last fifteen years.

But if you take a little time and dig a little deeper, when evaluating British tennis and the relative success of the LTA you arrive very quickly at the question... 'How can I NOT be successful?'

Given the prodigious amounts of money that the LTA, and more specifically Wimbledon, generates and given the incredible level of investment into British tennis over the last twenty or thirty years, to even begin to consider that winning the Davis Cup once in eighty years could be described as anything like success, is taking 'delusional' to a whole new level.

Firstly, let's look at the results from the matches played in the Davis Cup run in 2015. In their four ties against the USA, France, Australia and Belgium, Team GB played eighteen rubbers— fourteen singles, and four doubles. Of the eighteen rubbers, Andy Murray played eleven of them— eight singles and three doubles, winning them all. Of the balance seven matches, the rest of Team GB managed to win one; James Ward picking up a single victory against John Isner in the first-round tie.

So you could conclude that Andy Murray, as opposed to Team GB, won the Davis Cup! OK, I exaggerate to make a point, it's a team game and Andy needed his brother Jamie to win the three doubles matches, and without Wards' win in Glasgow, GB would have been knocked out in the first round. But the principle has some substance.

Britain has the third best record in the Davis Cup. We have won it ten times and finished runners-up eight times. Pretty impressive stuff. That is until you consider that sixteen of those final appearances were before 1937, and up until 1923, only five countries participated!

Let's look outside of the Davis Cup at our performance in world tennis in general.

In 1968, tennis became an 'Open Sport' and a new era of professional tennis players replaced what had been up until that point an entirely amateur sport. Since the open era started, there have been 304 Grand Slam finals across men's and women's singles. British players have contested 6% of them, winning seven (Andy Murray has won three and Virginia Wade won three; the last in 1977). Over the same period of time, the tennis powerhouse nations have obviously cleaned up right...the USA have won 135 titles and Australia has won 41. You would expect that, but look at some other countries more closely; Germany has won thirty-one titles, Sweden twenty-six titles, Spain twenty-seven titles, Switzerland twenty-four titles, Serbia twenty-three titles, Czech Republic nineteen titles, Russia twelve titles, and Argentina seven titles. This demonstrates just how poorly British tennis has performed over the last fifty years.

The numbers never lie...

Now it would be easy to find an excuse as to why. It would almost be possible to claim that seven titles are a positive achievement and that we rank ahead of France and Italy, both hotbeds of tennis culture. But let's get real here. Momentum is created by aligning three specific resources behind a clear objective. *Financial resource*: in 2014, the LTA invested over £70m in British tennis and has invested sums of this magnitude every year for decades. *Physical resource*: in a 2012/2013 Tennis Europe report, there was mention of the fact that Britain had 21,000 tennis courts (some way behind USA/Germany and France but way ahead of Spain, Australia, and Italy). *Human resource*: the same report identified 4.4m tennis players in the UK; a similar figure to all the other major tennis playing countries. It's not a resource issue then, is it?

Without Andy Murray, Britain wouldn't just be a backwater of world tennis, it would be a tiny stagnant pond. In essence, Murray has been successful in spite of the LTA. At fifteen, Murray moved to Barcelona to study at the Schiller International School and to train on the clay courts of the Sanchez-Casal Academy. He grew up with Rafa Nadal and benefited from the Spanish system. He has expressed strong opinions on the LTA and its effectiveness for him and others.

The difference between a successful person and others is not a lack of strength, not a lack of knowledge but rather in a lack of Will
-Vince Lombardi

If you read some of the press conference comments after the Davis Cup win, Murray is damning in his views on the LTA, how they have mismanaged tennis in Britain, failed to capitalize on his success; regularly change their plans, people, and objectives; created a £40m white elephant NTC in Roehampton, and destroyed the nucleus of promising junior players we once had. His final quote from the press conference is perhaps more damning than anything. he described conversations with Michael Downey the CEO of the LTA as a 'Waste of time. Nothing ever gets done.'

So what conclusion can we reach from these numbers and reflection on where British tennis is right now?

For me, there is only one: no one at the LTA has successfully answered the question yet 'how can I NOT be successful' ...it has systemically failed to deliver against its strategic objectives for fifty years, has systemically underperformed its potential, and has systemically wasted its valuable resource with fundamentally flawed planning and processes. Without being party to the inner workings of the LTA, it's pretty obvious from the outside that as an organisation it has more than its fair share of 'not successful' attributes: delusional, procrastination, short on motivation and commitment, does not have the right people making the right decisions, not finishing what they start, getting side-tracked, constantly changing the plan, and failing to invest in the right parts of the plan.

During the period 2009-2013, £26.4m was granted to British cycling from Sport England. In case you are struggling to work it out, that's roughly £6m per year; slightly less than the £70m the LTA invests and yet look at the output and results!

I wonder where tennis would be right now if Peter Keen in 1997 had been a tennis coach instead of a road racer?

Interestingly, in Sept 2015, Downey appointed Keen to the position of performance director of the LTA, on an interim basis, and the initial response from the tennis world was positive. In May 2016, Keen announced that he would not be extending his contract beyond the one-year term, leaving Downey in the position of having to find a performance solution for the third time in his three-year tenure. It will be intriguing to see how that plays out.

How can I NOT be successful?

As a personal aside here, for a number of years I worked in the tennis sector, running the UK business for the sports and racket brand Head. I had the opportunity to get up close and personal with most of the leading British players of the time and lots of the high-potential development players coming through. What I saw shocked me beyond the core. I was schooled in professional sport, schooled in high-performance results and I had never seen such a relaxed, lackadaisical, low-intensity, lazy group of professional athletes. They spent more time lying around drinking coffee than they did practising or training.

I wonder what Sir Dave Brailsford would have made of them?

Only by understanding what is holding you back will you be able to identify clearly in the next step how and what the right strategic choices are. The numbers tell you some of what you need to know, the people in your organisation tell you some of what you need to know, and the analysis of whether your organisation is truly aligned and cohesive will add another layer of insight. The final step is to identify any of the 'not successful' attributes that have pervaded your organisation.

What has stopped us being successful so far

Action -

- Take a good look at the business and form a view on whether you are deluding yourself or not.
- How sharp and relevant is your product offer?
- Are you focused enough on your customers and making them king?
- Do you invest enough of the right resources into the right areas?
- Are your team good enough (including you!)?
- Do you have a 'just do it' culture and is there sufficient *desire, belief,* and *commitment* to ride out the tough times?

OK, let's recap the key action points of Step One of our programme before we move on to making the right strategic choices.

What are the numbers really telling us?

Action -

- Focus on the numbers, understand what they are telling you, and never kid yourself it will just get better.
- Identify what your key performance indicators are and track their progress over a given period.
- Look at your sector and competitors to understand what good or great could look like.
- Identify the performance shift required to deliver outstanding results and performance.
- Bin the rose-coloured spectacles and be harsh with yourself and your team.

What is being said around the business that I need to know?

Action -

- Make sure that you and your senior executive team spend time at the coalface.
- Get out and listen to the people at the sharp end of your business.
- Go talk to customers and clients and get a real perspective of how it feels to them.
- Set up robust feedback mechanisms so that you can clearly articulate the temperature of your organisation.

How aligned is the organisation behind the plan?

Action -

- Develop a clear understanding of alignment in your organisation: is everyone pulling in the same direction?
- Make sure all the functions are aligned behind a common goal: is the effort harmonised?
- Are you sure that you have the three key resources—human, physical, financial— truly aligned behind the key initiatives?
- Have you removed the opposite forces and can you increase the mass behind the velocity?

What has stopped us being successful so far?

Action -

- Take a good look at the business and form a view on whether you are deluding yourself or not.
- How sharp and relevant is your product offer?
- Are you focused enough on your customers and making them king?
- Do you invest enough of the right resources into the right areas?
- Are your team good enough (including you!)?
- Do you have a 'just do it' culture and is there sufficient *desire, belief,* and *commitment* to ride out the tough times?

We have completed the deep dive into the business and how it looks and feels right now. It's probably been a brutal process— self-reflection always is. It's important at this stage to share the feedback and analysis with all the team who are going to be part of the next stage. Common understanding is a powerful component part of creating momentum in Steps Two to Five.

**In Step Two: we will provide you with a set of tools to get to
the right strategic choices; to test them before you decide, and
also to help you to pick what not to do**

Now bear with me for a few paragraphs while I get a little nostalgic.
Let's head back to the summer of 1979. I had turned eighteen and for
the first time could drink legally in a pub. Trevor Francis became the
first £1m footballer, signing for Nottingham Forest and going on to
score the winning goal in that year's European Cup Final; Tim Martin
opened his first JD Weatherspoon pub in Haringey, Elton John became
the first Western artist to perform live in the Soviet Union, there was a
Scottish devolution referendum, the Jubilee Line opened, McDonald's
launched the Happy Meal, Sony launched the Walkman, the world
premiere of Star Trek: the Motion Picture was held at the Smithsonian
Institute in Washington DC, and, probably most notably, Britain elected
its first female prime minister, Margaret Thatcher.

So what does all that have to do with you making the right strategic
choices? 'Not much' is the answer unless you choose to reflect on Tim
Martin and McDonald's apparently making a better strategic choice
than Sony did. However, one other thing happened in 1979, which has
shaped all subsequent business strategy: Michael Porter published his
first article, 'How competitive forces shape strategy,' in the Harvard
Business Review and spawned a whole new library of experts keen to
impress their views and beliefs on already confused business leaders.

From Porter's revolutionary beginning, every month brings us another
'latest and greatest' strategy book or the 'new world strategic thinking'
article. If you have enough time to study and read all these amazingly
erudite and believable tomes, isn't it fascinating how in some way they
all seem to subtly contradict each other? Reread these masterpieces
and how often do you see the shining example used at that point in
time (think Fannie Mae and David Maxwell getting the 'right people on

the bus' in Jim Collins excellent book *From Good to Great*) appear as the Emperor's new clothes a few years down the line, time after time.

Now I am not sitting here trying to convince you not to read anything—quite the opposite; I believe that all these great books have valuable insights that we as business leaders should and must take advantage of. What I very firmly believe, though, is don't let it over-complicate your process of making the right strategic choices.

Remember one key thing, the authors of most of these heavyweight strategic management business books are usually academics, unless it is a 'my life' read never lose sight of the fact that they are often predicting the past, and you need to become world class at predicting the future.

Strategy without tactics is the slowest route to victory.
Tactics without strategy is the noise before defeat.
-Sun Tzu

Back to beer then; I have never had the opportunity to meet Tim Martin, but I hope one day that I get the chance. It would be fascinating to sit and listen to his approach to business strategy. Weatherspoons has become an eponymous site on every high street in Britain; it has operated in one of the harshest sectors UK business has, with huge gorilla competitors, through how many down-cycle recessions of the economy and yet, in 2017, thirty-eight years later, the business is still thriving. Maybe, just maybe, Tim is a devout follower of Michael Porter, but my sense is probably not. As with lots of really successful entrepreneurs he gets the basics right and gives his customers what they want.

Step 2 now focuses on how to identify and build the new plan, and there are two parts to making the right strategic choices: *what* and *why*. I urge you not to lose sight of the equal importance of both. Typically, as business leaders at this stage, we start to focus on the *what* and then transition quickly into *how* - the doing stage: let's get started, make it happen, kick things off, etc.— we all know and use the language. At this stage, though, let's breathe and take a step back and as part of the process be really clear about *why*.

The *Why* part of Step 2, has two distinct benefits: it will help us to sense check our conclusion from the *what* part and challenges us to be sure it will it give us a position of competitive differentiation. It will also provide us with the narrative when we get to Step 5 and start to communicate the plan for our bright new world.

However, first, let's start with *what* at this point.

Fundamentally, if we strip out lots of the complications, I see there being three distinct options when you start to look at the right strategic choices for your business. Either i) **do something new** (read *Blue Ocean Strategy* if you want a sense of just how hard this is to pull off); ii) **react opportunistically to emerging possibilities** (read *Judo Strategy* if you want to see how to take advantage of an online niche); or iii) **build on what you already do well** (read *Hardball: five killer strategies for trouncing the competition* if you want to see how to get really aggressive).

Remember, this is your plan and these are your choices; no one else can make the decisions for you. So it's no good looking in the book for the right answer, it is inside your business; It is the insight you gained from Step One and the work you are about to do in Step Two; It is your knowledge of your sector, market, customers, trends, and opportunities. Package them all together and you will build a new set of strategic choices that drive the success you desire. If however you are looking for a clue right now, in my experience, the bold new plan will usually incorporate an element of the three distinct options: i) build on what you already do; ii) react opportunistically to changes and emerging opportunities; and iii) try some new things that might just work. It is possible to get a balance across the three without exposing the business to high risk or betting the house on a crazy scheme.

Now let's look at the *why* part of making the right strategic choices.

Vision - Purpose - Ambition

The WHY tool that I have used at a number of companies I have run has been VPA.

- **Vision** - where do we want to get to and what do we want to become?

- **Purpose** - why do we have a right to exist? What value are we adding that in our absence wouldn't be there?

- **Ambition** - what would success look like and by when?

Using this model, or a variant of this, as you start to formulate the right strategic choices, will challenge your assumptions and conclusions. It then has a secondary, but no less significant benefit: you can translate it into a very simple *why* message to communicate to the wider organisation. This is beneficial as we progress into Step 5 and start thinking about mobilising the troops.

When you write out your statement that expresses your vision and purpose, keep it as simple as you can; this is not the time for stuffy 'mission statements' that no one can remember. Make it a succinct expression of your aspiration for the business; use language that everyone can understand and relate to; use words that are simple, aspirational, and memorable and which will ultimately get your teams to buy into the vision as this will be one of the biggest success factors for the future.

We have all read lots of vision statements, and I don't plan to list hundreds of them here, but I will provide a couple of examples from brands that I think nail it.

One of my favourites is Harley-Davidson's, which is an expression of their vision and purpose all rolled into one.

Fulfilling dreams of personal freedom is more than a phrase.
(This is, in essence, their vision)
It's our purpose and our passion.
We bring a commitment of exceptional customer experiences to everything we do - from the innovation of our products to the precision of our manufacturing - culminating with our strong supplier and dealer networks. (In essence, this is their purpose)
We are Harley-Davidson.

Harley has a unique position in their statement of creating personal freedom and delivering an exceptional customer experience. If you visit their website, visit a dealership, test ride a bike, or talk to one of their staff, every picture, every word, and every expression is about personal freedom and the experience. There is a consistency in everything they do, which reinforces both internally and externally their differentiation.

The following one is from an eyewear retailer I discovered on a trip to the US. They are called Warby Parker, their vision, and their purpose read as follows:

> *Warby Parker was founded with a rebellious spirit and a lofty objective: to offer designer eyewear at a revolutionary price, while leading the way for socially conscious businesses.*
> (In essence, this is their vision)
>
> *'We believe that buying glasses should be easy and fun. It should leave you happy and good-looking, with money in your pocket,'*
> (In essence, their purpose)

If you go into a Warby Parker store or shop online with them, they make it fun. They have great advice and every time you buy a pair of glasses from them, they partner with VisionSpring and make a pair of glasses available to one of the one billion people in the world who need glasses but don't have them.

Also, from a big business, IKEA:

> *At IKEA, our vision is to create a better everyday life for the many people.*
>
> *Our business idea supports this vision by offering a wide range of well-designed, functional home furnishing products at prices so low that as many people as possible will be able to afford them.*
> (In essence, their purpose)

Think about IKEA, about how consistent they have been over the years; everything reflects the words and expressions of the VPA. 'For the many people' is a big statement and needs a big car park; they always have one. It needs a big store; they always have one. It needs a big choice; they always have one. 'Functional, at prices so low, many people can afford them' is another big purpose, but they never miss do they, even in the restaurants with their meatballs!

The real key to making *vision, purpose* and *ambition* work is to create uniqueness and then in everything you do throughout the organisation remain true and consistent to the vision and the purpose.

In each example above, the vision statement is something that customers, consumers, and staff can engage and identify with. Your success in building this powerful engagement across all your key stakeholders will ultimately be either one of the defining factors of sustained success or in living in a sea of mediocrity.

Similarly, the purpose statements of the three examples above provide real clarity on what world class competitive uniqueness or differentiation really looks like. Ask yourself this question: if my business wasn't here, what is it we offer that the customer would not be able to get anywhere else? If you can answer the question with a compelling conviction you have a shot at your summit. If you can't answer it or your answer is just wishy-washy, then ultimately you are selling a commodity and at some point, someone will cut your legs off.

Harley-Davidson is obvious from both the product and the brand positioning perspective: being a Harley owner clearly means something whether you decide to tattoo or not! Also, think about your shopping experience at IKEA: if it didn't exist and there wasn't a store in your area where would you go to get the choice, value and breadth of offer? There isn't anywhere. That's why both have endured for so many years and will continue to do so for many more to come.

The final part of the *why* is 'ambition'. This is simple and becomes your expression of what success looks like when you get to deliver your new world plan. It can be anything you want it to be: number-driven, experience-driven, values-driven, etc. It is entirely up to you to decide. When attempting to answer this, I have always asked myself one question: what would success look like when we get there, and then I've summed that up as the ambition.

Now, Step 2 of our programme will provide you with a set of tools to get to the right strategic choices, to test them before you decide, and also to help you to pick what not to do.

When I started out on the formative steps of my business career, after finishing as a golf professional, I had a number of jobs, mostly with retail and consumer-facing organisations. House of Fraser, Beales store group, Head Sports and then in 1994 I think it was, I joined a great British brand and company called Vango as sales director. Back then, and probably still to this day, Vango makes the best camping tents that money can buy. This was my first real sales job, working alongside the Silver Fox, Jim Murray a legend of the industry and a man who taught me loads about selling and marginally more about drinking whisky. I remember going to see the buyers at the Scouts retail business and having to pitch nearly fifteen huge tents in a field next to their offices. Boy, it was hard work. It was a hot summer, and as Jim was nearing retirement, somehow, it fell to the new guy to do most of the work.

That year I learned so much about pitching tents— some of which has probably saved my life on the big climbs I have done— but also learned so much about strategy, which I didn't realise at the time. For any business leader who has never been out on the road selling their business to new and existing clients, then my recommendation right here, right now, is get out of the ivory tower today, get some samples or brochures and go do some cold, or at best, lukewarm-calling. If you have a retail business, work the weekend in a store; if it's manufacturing, go sell some components. You have to understand what reaction you get when you pitch your brand or business proposition, how commercial it is, and how distinct.

During the summer of '94, I often idly ruminated on what kind of a salesperson I would choose to be if it was not tents, and I came to the conclusion that it would be best being a lace salesman. Clearly, this was motivated by the ease of carrying and presenting samples and not by any sector insight leading me to see laces as a blue ocean opportunity.

I would also ruminate on what would be the hardest sales job to have, and I finally settled on eggs. Can you imagine being sales director of an egg company? How do you differentiate an egg? Every single one looks exactly the same no matter the chicken; impossible to distinguish by colour or aesthetic until someone perfects the *'unbreakable in the carton until you get it home shell.'* There is no way to differentiate by technology. Unless you can turbocharge a chicken, it's hard to see how you can modernise the supply chain. You could try branding the packaging but how many designs of egg carton can you describe? The bottom line is that competitive differentiation in the egg world is challenging.

So we start Step 2 with a real hard look at what we are selling and why should someone buy our eggs. Let's be clear about what our brand and business proposition is going to be and where in the middle is our competitive point of differentiation. I see lots of companies get lost in the process at this stage, which is tough because this piece is probably the single most important part of running a business. Articulating the strategic choice of *what* you are selling and *why*, is challenging. Making it unique is the *win* part.

You need to find ways to test the assumptions that you make and test the conclusions that you reach. You need a reasonable market insight and a broad feel for what's happening out there. You need a strong sense of what you are good at and where the best opportunities await. Don't get suckered into the latest management or strategic thinking at this point; keep it simple. Decide which mix of the three strategic options you are going to pursue. Be clear about why and start to make your choices.

Now not many business books will have ever transitioned seamlessly from egg cartons to Harley-Davidson motorbikes, but I am about to try. The story of this iconic brand is worth spending time looking at. I cannot claim any responsibility for their success, but if you look at the journey the business has been through you will see many similarities between their journey and the process you are embarking on right now.

The Harley-Davidson story

The birth of the Harley-Davidson legend began in 1903, in a small shed in the Davidson family backyard in Milwaukee.

It started with Walter Davidson's ambition, 'to be the best bicycle rider' and over the next 100+ years has turned into a thriving multibillion-dollar global brand. Walter, and Arthur Davidson, along with their long-time friend William S. Harley, developed the idea of building an engine into a bicycle. Aged 21, Harley wrote the blueprint and the team spent many hours, without success, trying to perfect the power cycle. Initial prototypes could not handle the hills around Milwaukee without pedal assistance, and eventually, they moved on from bicycles and started to develop the world's first motorcycle. Over a year later the first Harley bike, the Serial Number One, became the first production Harley motorcycle available to the public and the journey began.

By 1907, they had one full-time employee, and they sold 150 motorcycles, with their biggest customer being the local Police Force.

The Davidsons and Harley were always trying out innovations to make their motorcycles better and faster. In 1908, the reputation of the company was elevated further when Walter's new V-Twin-engine bike, generating seven horsepower (double any other bike around) won some local race meetings. Production increased to 1500 bikes by 1909, and further product development reinforced the brand's position as the market leader in motorcycles. During the First World War the US Army ordered over 15,000 Harley Davidsons and by 1918, Harley-Davidson became the world's largest motorcycle company producing 28,000 motorcycles.

The Harley motorbike not only looked different, but it also sounded different. The growl of the Harley engine was, and still probably is the single biggest selling factor, described as 'a voice: a bassoprofundo thump that makes other motorcycles sound like sewing machines.' It is a pure expression of testosterone.

By the mid-1950s, Harley-Davidson became the undisputed leader of the motorcycle market. Its bikes were advertised in magazines and promoted mainly by word of mouth. Harley bikes were used by the U.S. military, highway patrol officers, Hell's Angels, and Hollywood rebels, who all loved the rugged, tough image their bike portrayed. The iconic actors of the time, James Dean and Marlon Brando would regularly be photographed astride a Harley, complete with dangling cigarette and cool shades.

In the late 1950s, this roster expanded to include young 'Elvis types' attracting dates with their Harley motorcycles. Given this customer base, Harley's brand imagery would often depict leather-clad riders or police officers on motorcycles. These images cultivated a reputation of Harley motorcycles as tough, rugged machines. Associated with people who were willing to break the traditional mould or reflected rugged individuality and the frontier spirit of the United States.

Although Harley-Davidson was successful in positioning itself as one of the leading motorbike brands, the company consistently faced an image problem. Harley riders were stereotyped as 'pot-smoking, beer-drinking, woman-chasing, tattoo-covered, leather-clad bikers.'

In 1965, in an effort to expand production and raise capital for new products, the firm went public after sixty years of private ownership. This proved to be an ill-fated move and by 1969, the company was faced with a shortfall of cash and confronted by new and severe pressure from competitors. That year, Harley-Davidson was acquired in a friendly takeover by AMF, a heavy-industrial conglomerate looking to diversify into leisure products.

AMF slashed the workforce and streamlined production, resulting in labour strikes and a lower-quality product. In the following period, through the 70s and into the 80s, Harley-Davidson started to struggle. The world of motorbikes was changing, new Japanese brands (Honda, Yamaha, Suzuki, Kawasaki) were coming into the US market, producing lighter weight, lower cost, more fuel-efficient motorcycles. The younger generation of riders embraced these new brands and new products; they required little or no maintenance, were easier to handle and ride, were quieter and didn't have the negative stereotype connotations of owning a Harley. Between 1970 and 1980, Harley-Davidson's share declined by over 80%.

The numbers never lie...

In 1981, AMF sold their shareholding to a group of 13 investors for $80m. By 1983, the company was in survival mode again, teetering on the edge of bankruptcy, and the board of Harley-Davidson was forced to reconsider their overall strategy. Two of the company's senior executives, Vaughan Beals, vice president of motorcycle sales, along with Willie G. Davidson, grandson of the company founder, made an inspired decision. These two leaders decided to leave the ivory tower and drive to Harley-Davidson rallies across America to meet their customers, learn from the complaints or concerns they had with their machines, and listen to what was getting said in the trenches.

The brand's loyal followers, known as HOGs (Harley Owners Group), were the forefront leaders of this movement and were vociferous with their feedback on product quality, product suitability, and brand positioning. The Board responded to everything they heard, drawing up a new strategic plan and making their set of strategic choices that defined a bright new world for both the Harley workers and the Harley owners.

As we saw in Step Two with the vision and purpose, the starting point of the new world was to recognise that rather than trying to sell motorbikes into a changing market, rather than trying to sell quantity instead of focusing on quality, rather than trying to compete with the Japanese instead of owning a niche, Harley had lost its way. The enlightened board drew up a vision statement, which is still remarkably close to the current one they have today.

We fulfil dreams inspired by the many roads of the world, providing extraordinary motorcycles and customer experiences.
We fuel the passion for freedom in our customers to express their individuality.

They realised that differentiation would come from building on their core foundation. A combination strategy of focusing on the core and differentiation from competitors would provide the greatest chance of survival.

So they set about being the best at what they were good at, making motorbikes that were unique in delivering extraordinary customer experiences. They focused on building the Harley-Davidson community, the owners group, as their core brand proposition. However, they also committed to change from the historic 'Hells Angels, bad boy biker image' and transitioned into a more premium upmarket owners club.

They started to sponsor events and rides out. They introduced test ride facilities. They built a network of their own dealerships that all set up their own local Harley chapters. They established academies of motorcycling to teach members to ride a Harley. They succeeded in attracting a new customer segment, otherwise known as Rubbies (Rich urban bikers). These riders helped bring back Harley-Davidson into market dominance. Research by the Wall Street Journal stated that 'one in three of today's Harley-Davidson buyers are professionals or managers.' Within a few years, the majority of Harley riders were in their mid-40s, earned over $100,00, 30% had college degrees, and an astonishing 50% of owners were repeat purchasers— the lifeblood of any brand.

Membership of the HOGs now numbers many multiple millions around the world. The company spends little on traditional advertising, preferring to use its marketing spend to drive both emotional attachments to the brand and engagement with the customer experience. Bear in mind that this strategy was conceived in 1983, fully two decades before many other brands had started talking about community and emotional engagement. If you get a chance, take a look at the Harley website to see really how compelling the customer experience and sense of community is these days.

In isolation, this would not have been enough; they recognised that improving company profitability was also a must. So they set about on a radical overhaul of their manufacturing processes. Introducing MAN (materials as needed), transitioning to a more democratic leadership style where all workers on the production line were given more autonomy, and focusing on build quality rather than production-line quantity. They succeeded in re-establishing quality as a core attribute but also producing some stunning product standards. Between 1981 and 1988, inventory was reduced by 67%, productivity increased by 50%, scrap and rework went down by two-thirds, and defects per unit decreased by 70%. Harley-Davidson restored profitability to above industry standard and for an extended period, the company's share price consistently outperformed Wall Street.

The company's CEO at the time and the man recognised as leading the strategy change, Richard Teelink—demonstrating transformational leadership in an era when control and command were still the main styles in manufacturing all over the world— is quoted as saying:

'The biggest takeaway is that positive change will happen as long as you don't try to force yours. If you lead participative change, it will work.'

Next, Harley started to look at the product and how to stay core but also innovate. Firstly, they recognised that being part of a growing community would influence Harley owners to want to customise their bikes and demonstrate the answer to the question of, 'How do I become part of the community but also demonstrate my uniqueness?' They launched a programme where customers could design and have built they own bikes, blending their personality into the bike's **customised look** by choosing custom paint, custom seats, wheels, and all the metalwork. They can **customise** *fit*, selecting seats, suspension, handlebars, and foot controls. They can **customise** *function*, choosing racks, backrests, windshields, and luggage and finally, they can **customise** *performance*, selecting exhausts, intakes, and stage kits.

These days, when we buy a new car, our expectation is that we have a high degree of customisation options. Big fashion brands like Nike are working diligently to make trainer customisation a point of difference for their youth consumers, but we are talking Harley-Davidson customisation here in the mid-80s; unheard of when the Japanese bike and car companies were solely focused on driving down unit manufacturing cost.

Harley also addressed the lighter-weight sports bike market and introduced a new technology, by breaking from sixty-five years of tradition and creating the V-Rod; a new generation of Harley riders was born. In early 2005, Harley launched a second bike as part of the V-Rod family, which it named the Street-Rod. The company also redesigned its Sportster family of entry-level, lower-priced bikes in 2004 to appeal to younger riders and women riders. With prices starting at $6,500, the company was attempting to position the new Sportster within the grasp of a younger group of riders, and women whom it hoped would grow loyal to the Harley-Davidson brand.

The final part of the new world plan was to diversify into two areas: financial services, which was, in essence, providing the funding for Harley owners to buy their bikes, insurance, roadside assistance, and extended warranties; and lifestyle products and branded merchandise, a clothing and accessories line that now contributes over $300m to global revenue.

Over the last thirty years, undoubtedly things will have changed, things will have worked, things will have failed, people will have come, and people will have gone. The new strategy encompassed all three strategic options:

- **Do something new**: community and customisation;

- **Take advantage of emerging possibilities:** financial services and lifestyle products;

- **Build on what you do well:** lead the world in high quality, heavyweight touring bikes, with a crystal clear *vision* and *purpose*.

In 2014, the financial performance was stellar; net income was $850m, up 16% on total global revenue of $6.3b, which was up 7%. For full-year 2014, Harley shipped 270,726 motorcycles to dealers and distributors, which was a 3.9% increase compared to 2013. Retail unit sales for 2014 were up 1.3% in the US, 11.8% in the Asia-Pacific region, 6.4% in the EMEA region, and 2.1% in the Latin America region.

The Numbers Never Lie…

Here's how Keith Wandell, chairman, president, and CEO of Harley-Davidson, summed it up: 'Harley-Davidson achieved a great year of financial performance in 2014, with double-digit earnings growth, revenue topping $6 billion and continued strong improvement in margins. We also continued to broaden our customer base and expand the reach of our brand through unrivalled products and experiences. In international markets, our dealers in Asia Pacific, EMEA, and Latin

America posted their highest new motorcycle sales on record for each region, delivering on our expectation for international sales to grow at a faster rate than US sales. And in the US, for the third straight year, sales to our outreach customers grew at more than twice the rate of sales to core customers.'

I'll finish this section with my two favourite Harley observations. Firstly, how many brands do you know where their customer base considers tattooing the name across visible parts of the body as a sign of their commitment to the HOG community and their particular chapter? It's incredible! Secondly, take a look at the Harley-Davidson website and click on the button marked leadership. Whereas in most $6 billion corporations you would have a tonne of Suits smiling back at you, at Harley-Davidson, they all wear leather biker jackets...awesome!

One final footnote on the journey that Harley-Davidson have been through and lots of lessons to learn from. They were clear about what their brand and business proposition was going to be and where in the middle their competitive point of differentiation lay. They have remained steadfastly consistent with their original strategy, developing, refining, and augmenting as they have gone along but never deviating far from the plan. They have had ups and downs but have continued to flourish in the long term and built a solid base for the future. They have delivered a masterclass in how to make the right strategic choices, drive enhanced business performance, and deliver sustainable success.

As Keith Wandell puts it, 'Our success is the result of a clear focus on managing the company for the long term, building on our well-established strategies, and driving continuous improvement in every aspect of our business.'

Identify your unique point of competitive positioning and define your VPA

Action -

- Articulate exactly what your brand and business proposition is going to be.
- Describe your vision, purpose, and ambition clearly.

- Establish what your customer couldn't get anywhere else if you didn't exist; set it in the context of the market you plan to attack.
- Define your point of competitive differentiation.
- Understand that it's probably not going to be a radical strategy but be ready to identify how you will win.
- Be clear about what you are going to do differently.

Control what you can control

On 4 November 2008, I landed at Paris CDG airport on my way back from a trip to see our Berghaus business in Asia. I caught up with two key stories unfolding at the time: the election of Barak Obama as the first African-American President of the United States and, following that, the continued fallout from the bankruptcy of Lehman Brothers and the financial destruction caused by the collapse of the US property and subprime mortgage markets. A week later, I was making the opening presentation at the Berghaus International sales launch to our global partner base, and I distinctly remember using a slide that said, 'The world will never be the same again. What we experience now is the new norm... deal with it.'

The economic shift we experienced over the next twelve months was probably unprecedented; for those of us running businesses at the time, it most definitely was. The world changed and all the rules and guidelines we had steadfastly adhered to for so many years disappeared. I remember sitting in countless meetings trying to decide what we would do if the Euro (as was expected at the time) also collapsed as a consequence of the sovereign debt crisis.

What struck me at the time was the scale and the magnitude of some of the issues we were wrestling with. Complex solutions were way beyond my pea-brain capability, and yet as we went through our annual strategic planning process, I was leading a Board who were trying to figure out what to do with these enormous issues.

Then something else struck me...why bother?

I figured somewhere in the world, someone much cleverer than me would be trying to sort the mess out and if they were struggling then why was I wasting my valuable time also trying to find an answer. When you are defining your business strategy you need to be cognisant of two important 'big picture' points;

- What's happening out there?

- How might it shape the sector or arena that we operate in?

Let me give you a 'here and now' example. As I finish this book, Britain has just voted to Leave the European Union and within a couple of years, what has been dubbed Brexit will be a reality. We will no longer be a member of the EU. Now, in the history of Britain, this will live as one of the single most important passages of our time. However, the question for us as business leaders should not be to radically reconstruct our strategic planning, it is to work out how this might shape our sector and figure out how Leave shapes our commercial reality.

There is no way can you solve the issues that will arise from Brexit. Yes, take some time out to think through how the changes may shape your sector at a macro level; then spend more time focused on how you benefit from the shift in the environment as we discussed in Step One.

Will a weakening of sterling provide a short-term opportunity to build a stronger export position for your business? Yes, for sure. Will there be other short-term impacts on the economy, currency movements, property values, availability of cash for investment, etc.? Yes, for sure. Could you articulate them all now? Somehow, I doubt it. Will there be a shift in availability of a lower cost workforce, possibly? The government will negotiate a new trading agreement with the EU; they will now be able to negotiate new arrangements directly with other world powers; China, US, Russia, Brazil, etc. Ultimately, the global economy for Britain will not change that much. Does this provide a new strategic choice for you?

Britain survived and flourished as an independent country for many hundreds of years; we led the development of the modern world; we are still the fifth-biggest global economy. We already have our own currency. We have a strong trading position with the major EU countries. We are one of France's largest export markets for wine and cheese and a huge consumer of German cars and white goods. Things will not change that much. Market forces will not let it happen.

Control what you can control...

But don't get hooked up on trying to figure out too much. Of far greater value to your strategic thinking is to stay closer to home and look at the trends, key influences, and demographics that immediately impact your business. By the time you have figured out the big stuff, it will all have changed anyway. Focus on controlling what you can control. Make your strategic choices about you and your core competencies. Build into your thinking factors that need to be changed and be clear that you have sufficient power to control the change. Use the big trends as you see them as indicators, as directional arrows, not as rip-it-up-and-start-again instructions.

Focus on the areas that you have the power to control

Action -

- identify the big picture trends that could impact your sector in the medium term.
- Be clear about what the core competencies of your organisation are.
- Articulate how you will change the value chain to adapt to the shift in strategic intent.
- Detail where you want to play and how you will win.
- Understand the impact of time on your plan.

At 6 pm on 24 September 1975, Doug Scott and Dougal Haston staggered up the final slopes of Everest's Southeast Ridge and became the first two Brits to stand on top of the world's highest mountain. They had also become the first climbers to ascend by the south-west face, in a classic siege-style expedition led by Sir Chris Bonington.

For Chris, this was the culmination of many years planning and building a strategy to become part of the first expedition to climb the south-west face of Everest. Five previous expeditions (including his own British attempt in 1972) had tried it and all failed. Beaten back by harsh conditions and a seemingly unclimbable rock band— a massive wall of limestone spanning the width of Everest with 1,000 ft. vertical cliffs. With this in mind, Sir Chris decided his expedition would go left, and try to force the previously unclimbed rock band via a deep gully, opening an alternative route to the summit. This was successfully achieved using expert technical climbing techniques. On 22 September the expedition reached Camp 6, their final camp before the summit, and he and his team had reached their goal.

Sir Chris is an amazing man and a great friend who I have been so lucky to climb with. He is an inspirational leader, a brilliant strategist, and someone who has taught me so much about life and how to succeed in business. His most powerful lessons, however, have all been around... 'Can you walk the talk or climb Everest the *hard way*?'

If you ever fancy reading a climbing book, my recommendation is pick up a copy of *Everest the Hard Way* and settle in for an incredible adventure. In it, he talks about having the dream of climbing the south-west face of Everest—doing something that no one had done before— and he walks you through one of the fundamental parts of building strategy, how to align resource requirements and capability behind strategic intent.

The unsuccessful south-west face expedition of 1972, which Chris had also led, taught him a lot and after raising significant funding from Barclays Bank he returned in '75 to finish the job. He arrived with a new plan. He had considered all the critical success factors and shaped his resources accordingly. Complete with computer analysis for stocking and assaulting the mountain, he implemented a raft of changes identified at the end of the first climb.

Failure is the opportunity to start again more intelligently

The raft of changes included the following: arriving earlier, moving Camp IV, putting netting above the MacInnes boxes to dispel falling debris, and changing the route to scale the rock band that had previously thwarted all attempts. The weather behaved enough for the team to pretty much follow the strategy and they got enough gear high enough for two summit assaults. The two geniuses of the expedition, Doug Scott and Dougal Haston, made it to the top quite late in the day and were forced to snow-hole bivouac near the South Summit.

The true heroes of the expedition, though, were Nick Estcourt and Tut Braithwaite. Sir Chris had identified these two guys as being a critical resource with the required skillset to make the push through the rock band, thus making summit attempts possible. Estcourt and Tut duly achieved this while understanding their exertions would finish any chance they would have at a summit bid.

Leave the jersey in a better place than you found it

Running a big climbing expedition is so similar to running a business.

You start with the strategic choice: which mountain are we going to climb? You build your plan of attack: how will we get to the top? You look at your milestones or stage gates: where should we pitch our camps? And build a timing sequence of delivery: when do we need to get there to give ourselves the best chance of success? You start to build a financial model: how much investment will be required and where does the money come from?

You examine what physical tools will deliver you a better likelihood of success: what technology can we benefit from?

Then you focus on people, what skill sets, capabilities, and competencies do you need? Where are the gaps? And finally, build your what-if scenarios, so you are ready to handle some degree of adversity when you face it.

It is always further than it looks.
It is always taller than it looks.
And it is always harder than it looks. -
The three rules of mountaineering
(and business strategy)

The alignment of resource behind strategic intent is the absolute cornerstone of making the new plan work. All the great thinking will unravel at some point, just like the climbing expedition will fail if there is no focus on the right level of investment into the right areas of resource requirement.

Sir Chris is a master of walking the talk as his incredible list of first ascents is a testimony to. He was one of the original climbing strategists and leaders and played a lead role in changing the way expeditions climbed big mountains. If you ever get the chance to hear him speak, take it.

The JLP phenomena

One of the highlights of Christmas is always the first viewing of the new John Lewis advert. It has become a bit of a national institution and every year sends the internet into a frenzy when it is first released. The Man in the Moon ad for Christmas 2015 was viewed over twenty-four million times on YouTube alone, which is an astonishing statistic given that everything we read these days tells us consumers are no longer influenced by classic ATL media.

But then this is John Lewis and, over the last 150 years, I guess we have learned not to be surprised by anything they achieve.

John Lewis was founded in 1864 as a shop on London's Oxford Street selling goods such as Lyon silk and Calais lace and has grown to be one of the UK's best-loved companies. In the past year, it was named the most admired British company for honesty and trust in an Ipsos Mori survey and it regularly comes at or near the top of customer satisfaction surveys.

In truth, though, the early beginnings of the John Lewis empire were somewhat different.

Born in 1836 in Shepton Mallet, Somerset, John Lewis, the founder, was no industrial democrat. He was fired from his first job at a draper's in Liverpool after fighting with another employee, and this prompted Lewis to make his way to London, where he converted an Oxford Street tobacconist's into his first store. Being a store owner did little to dampen his competitive spirit. After refusing to comply with a court order not to change the facade of the store, Lewis spent three weeks in prison. Sir Edward Carson QC, the eminent barrister, and politician, appeared both for and against Lewis in court and said, 'I would be puzzled to say which position was the more difficult of the two.'

Lewis demonstrated little interest in the welfare of his workers. Eliza, his wife, said that his only belief was 'in the divine right of employers.' It was left to John Lewis's son, Spedan, to lay the foundation of the values and principles of the John Lewis Partnership, 'the way we do stuff around here' and create the ethos of JLP, which still endures to this day.

When he joined the business, Spedan was shocked to learn that he, his father and his brother were, between them, earning more than John Lewis's 300 employees put together. Peter Cox, a John Lewis historian and retired partner, wrote in his book *Spedan's Partnership: The Story of John Lewis and Waitrose*, that John Lewis had a fixed view of employees. 'Many of his workers were lazy, and only did the minimum they could get away with. Spedan's response was that since they had no stake whatever in the success of the business they gained nothing by extra effort.'

Spedan convinced his father to allow him to take control of the Peter Jones department store that the company had just acquired in London's Sloane Square and it was here that he would start to lay the foundation of the Partnership of today. At Peter Jones, Spedan tried out his new ideas: better pay and profit-sharing for all workers, a staff council, and the first editions of the JLP magazine The Gazette. In 1928, when his father died, Spedan took full control of the company and the following year signed an agreement handing over the business to be held in trust for all the staff. In essence at this point, everyone working for John Lewis became a partner. To be paid back out of future profits, he used an interest-free loan to fund the share transfer and in 1950, signed a second trust settlement, handing over his remaining controlling share to the partners in exchange for a promise that the company would continue to adhere to its democratic principles.

JLP now has 47 department stores around the UK, as well as owning Waitrose a thriving 300-store supermarket business. It prides itself and is widely seen, as being totally service-oriented, offering an excellent choice of high-quality brands and products, with good value at its core. Yes, its merchandise might be more premium than other stores, and therefore more expensive, but as a customer, you know that what it has is keenly priced. If you can buy the same product more cheaply at another high-street retailer, or on another high-street retailer's website the store will refund the difference. Like-for-like, John Lewis, famously, is 'never knowingly undersold.'

It is also the UK's largest employee-owned business and one of the most successful in the world. Its central purpose is painted on the wall of the Cambridge branch as you walk up the stairs from what, in any other company, would be the staff entrance. Here it is the partners' entrance. The 93,800 people who work in the business are called partners and John Lewis, to them, is not the company, it is the partnership.

Managers remind you of the partnership's purpose whenever they talk about the business. They have a feeling of ownership that is rarely found in other organisations. Does it influence them to deliver just a little bit more in the way of customer experience? Yes. All feedback from customers and surveys would indicate that a strong sense of ownership always delivers the little bit extra. 'The partnership's ultimate purpose is the happiness of all its members through their worthwhile and satisfying employment in a successful business.'

Start from *why*; have a clear purpose; your team will buy into it and deliver outstanding results.

Every year, all partners benefit from the success of the company, through a profit-share structure that regularly provides them with 15% of their annual salary in bonus. In addition to the annual bonus and discounts in the shops, partners and their families can stay, at a subsidised rate, at one of John Lewis's five UK holiday venues or sail on one of its five yachts on the Solent. Both are perks that reflect the JLP purpose!

It is a unique business. On the one hand, the staff own it and yet there is a senior executive team that runs and operates the company as if it was a typical independent entity. Yes, the partners are kept well informed about what is going on, but the exec team still make the big strategic decisions around direction and investment. This throws up some fascinating challenges around leadership and motivation, which we will come back to in Steps 4 and 5.

Many inside the company will say that the partnership structure has allowed JLP to think long term with its business plan and its capacity to invest and nowhere is this more visible than the journey that the store group has been on to develop an e-commerce and latterly an omnichannel capability.

In the very early 2000s, enlightened retailers were just starting to see that in some way the internet and the opportunity for consumers to shop online was about to begin. No one had any idea how big or how quickly or how much it would change the retail sector. Many chose to stay in denial, buried their heads in the sand, and hoped it would just go away. Many were real sceptics who never thought it would happen. Some chose to embrace the opportunity to trade online, seeing it as a true paradigm shift about to occur in the world of consumer spending. JLP was one of the enlightened ones.

In 2001, JLP bought a small online retail site, Buy.com. In October that year, it launched a new johnlewis.com transactional website using the platform it had inherited from buy.com, the first winter of trading delivered sales comparable to a small store, with the business transacting around 1000 orders a day in the run-up to Christmas. The cut-off for pre-Christmas delivery was 16 December, (interestingly some fifteen years on, there are still retailers out there with the same Christmas cut-off date!) and they delivered 99% of orders on time.

The plan back then was to invest between £30-40m in developing the online capability and that it would take three to four years to reach profitability.

Let's fast forward to 2010 and we see that from little acorns, sometimes large e-commerce shopping streams do grow!

In their 2010 review of progress, JLP announced that sales had reached £383m for the previous year. They, like many high-street retailers, had embraced the development of e-commerce, invested in it and were starting to see the future potential. At this stage, most retailers were still in the multiple-channel mode, seeing e-commerce as a stand-alone revenue stream and driving strategic activity accordingly. JLP, though, were clever at this stage and recognised a number of consumer trends that shaped thinking within the exec team.

They analysed the shopping habits of three distinct customer sets: their store-only customers, their online-only customers, and their multi-channel customers. Store customers shopped on average twice a year with John Lewis whereas a multi-channel customer purchased on average six times a year and spent 3.3x what a single-channel shopper would spend; powerful data. Recognising that if they invested and drove an integrated multi-channel strategy, they had enormous opportunity to increase customer lifetime value, the exec team built a new world strategic plan with online growth at the heart of it.

The first key step was to extend the 'never knowingly undersold' policy to the online business; this was a brave move and one that required a potential £50m investment in lost margin. At the same time, they launched free Wi-Fi in store, in effect making it easier for the customer to 'showroom' products and then search for a better price— a very brave move. The head of online delivery and customer experience, Sean O'Connor, indicated at the time that it had been a big step forward in helping customers make an informed purchase decision.

'They can quickly and easily access our mobile-optimised website, or use our iPhone app. Customers are free to access the whole of the web, including competitor sites to test our price commitment, however, it primarily enables us to extend our John Lewis online content and services into our physical shops in a way that is convenient for them'

The next step was to invest in a 'click and collect' service offer, which is challenging for a retailer more used to shipping bulk quantities to each store. Now a JLP customer could order online and pick up the next day from either a John Lewis or select Waitrose stores. The following year, 16% of total orders were collected from a store; by 2011, this had increased to 22%.

More investment followed in their product offerings, and SKU count increased from 100,000 to 200,000 with a big drive into the fashion sector— an area johnlewis.com had previously not been targeting. They invested in brand shops, Mulberry, Barbour, Ralph Lauren, Diesel and supported this with a whole raft of inspirational content from guest and leading fashion experts to support the drive.

More investment followed into their mobile site, after seeing the trend for multi-channel shoppers to research online, try in store, and complete the purchase on a desktop. In 2010, 100,00 customers were using their mobile site and looking at the site now, it was pretty basic but very forward thinking, and the company followed up quickly with an iPhone app and other technology solutions such as QR codes. By 2013, traffic to the mobile site (53%) overtook traffic to the desktop site.

Over the next three years, this new plan of targeted growth saw online sales doubled to £800m in FY 2012. But the exec team did not stop there; they circled back to our Step One, revisited where they were right now, looked at how the world of retail was changing and built a new... 'new world plan.'

In June 2012, long before it became a buzz word, Andy Street, the managing director of John Lewis stores, told the audience at the British Retail Consortium (BRC) Symposium event that John Lewis would be strongly pursuing an omnichannel strategy.

'The strategy's quite simple,' he explains. 'We know that about 60% of our customers buy both online and in shops so the approach is to make it absolutely seamless for them to move from one to the other. So they can research in one place and shop in the other, they can buy in one place and pick up in the other - the art of sales is consistent across channels, so the whole approach is to make it channel agnostic. They're not even supposed to know or see or realise which channel they're using because it's one overall customer offer.'

The shift to an integrated omnichannel strategy has required significant further investment in all areas of the business. Creating this seamless transaction requires back-office functions that deliver huge customer value but are not consumer facing. A new 650,00 sq. ft. distribution centre had been opened in 2008; this now had a further £100m spent on doubling capacity and by 2014 a total of £280m had been invested in ensuring that fulfilment delivered against customer expectation. The distribution centre now ships 400,000 orders per day. What a change from the days of 2002.

Investment in IT increased from 15% of the CapEx spend in the period 2009-2013, and it is forecast to increase to 37% 2014-2018. The front-end website was completely overhauled in February 2013 and is continually upgraded. There are now over 2000 staff employed solely on johnlewis.com technology. In 2013, the company set up JLAB, a business incubator for technology start-ups, investing capital, knowledge and mentoring in finding the new tools of the future. Each of the five selected start-ups gets twelve weeks and support to demonstrate their technology. The first winners of the £100,000 investment were an Australian beacon-technology company, and JLP is now trialling the tech solution to alert staff so that when a click-and-collect customer comes into a store, they arrive at the desk and their parcel is already there waiting for them... Cool!

By 2014, online sales topped £1.1 billion and were over a third of total JLP sales. Andy Street now forecasts that by 2019, online revenue will surpass store revenue, one year ahead of the original plan. But the reality is it does not matter because in a true omnichannel world there is only one revenue: customer revenue.

Interestingly, during this period of tremendous online growth, John Lewis have also continued to invest in their store portfolio. In 2002, they had 27 stores and by 2009 this had increased to 35. By the end of 2015, the number stood at 47. This is happening at a time when other retailers are actively shrinking their store base. Again, the driver of this strategy is omnichannel. Street identified back in 2009 when he opened the JLP store in Cardiff that the original thinking of an extended online offer would take John Lewis to potential customers out of a store reach, but quite the opposite happened. When a new store opened, in this instance Cardiff, online sales for customers within an hours' drive of the store went up by over 40%, reinforcing the strategic choices made.

Nowadays, John Lewis is held up in the UK as one of, if not THE leader in omnichannel customer service. Typically, we associate new business and start-ups with having the flexibility and the new world foresight to take advantage of the changing face of a sector; think Amazon or Asos as pure-play etailers who now dominate their world. Somehow the last business we would expect to be able to take advantage so successfully of such a paradigm shift in consumer behaviour would be a 150-year-old company, steeped in tradition, ingrained in bricks and mortar and run as a partnership.

If we drill a little further into the strategic choices made, somewhat like Harley-Davidson, we see a blend of the three options; **i) do something new**: broaden the product and brand offer moving into new revenue streams; **ii) take advantage of emerging possibilities**: target the growth of online shopping and a material shift in customer buying habits; and **iii) build on what you do well**: take great brands and products, never knowingly undersold, to a wider consumer base through more stores and JLP.com...all achieved with a crystal clear *vision* and *purpose*.

Mark Lewis, John Lewis's online director, believes that the company is only at the very beginning of its omnichannel journey. 'We've cleared the first hurdle,' he says. 'Now a number of us have built quite sizeable online businesses in the UK there's a temptation to think we're close to the end of this race,' he told delegates at a recent Internet Retailing Conference. 'But I think, if anything, we're at the very beginning of it. This journey is ahead of us rather than behind us. These next three to five years will see more changes to retail than in our generation.'

The JLP success is a tribute to three key things: interpreting the insight and data effectively and translating this into making the right strategic choices, understanding how to take advantage of the new world opportunity without straying from the core purpose and proposition of the company, but then also having the guts and the strength of character to invest in making the new plan successful. Invest in the key areas, aligning resource— human, physical and financial—directly behind strategic intent.

Investing ahead of the growth curve has created a market-leading position for JLP and one which is wholly defensible as the consumer sector changes over the next decade. It is amazing, really, when you look at the shift in their business over such a relatively short period of time. In the first 137 years, they built turnover across stores and supermarkets up to £4.4 billion. In the next thirteen years, this increased to £11 billion of which nearly £4 billion has come from online.

One final footnote on JLP, they now have a project group actively working to define what their world will look like in 2028, 100 years after Spaden Lewis inherited the business from his father. WOW!

Define the resource requirement for the new plan

Action -

- Start to align resource requirement—physical, human, and capital—with strategic intent.
- Map where the cash will come from and when you will need it.
- Understand what core competencies the strategy will need and spot the gaps.
- What are the critical success factors?
- Build in technology as an enabler.
- Be clear who your star climbers are, you will need them at some point.
- Plan for when it goes wrong and have a contingency

The rise and fall of the Hockey Stick
(Will it make money?)

Don't you just love accountants? I am serious. Don't you just love them?

Every year accountants are given the thankless task of preparing The Budget and every year, bless their little number-crunching hearts, they deliver—only to see their hard work go off the rails and into the ditch in under eight seconds. The derailment process starts when the bosses see the budget and react in horror and disbelief. In the corporate world, the CEO knows they cannot take *that* budget to the shareholders without risking them concluding that the management are incompetent spendthrifts.

So we always revert to a Goldilocks budget—not too big, not too small, just right—at least until after the financial plans for the new year have been approved and signed off. The dialogue between the bosses and the finance team invariably focuses on the assumptions underlying the numbers, and this makes sense because assumptions are not laws of physics and can be altered with a stroke of the accountant's red pen.

The debate usually goes like this: 'What do you mean [insert name of big customer who has struggled this year but is needed to grow again to fund the new budget] won't continue growing from here to eternity?' or 'What do you mean growth in [insert product category which has been in decline for years due to competitive pressure] isn't appropriate in these circumstances?'

However, when a CEO delivers a new strategic plan budget with his board of directors why do they always do it by presenting a chart known as the 'hockey stick'? The blade of the hockey stick sits down in the lower left-hand corner of the chart; this is the god-awful-horrible-results quadrant the business has just been through and is the justification for the new plan. The stick then swoops up hard and fast to the top right quadrant where revenues flow into the corporate coffers from all the new strategies and investments; everyone collects their bonuses and goes home happy.

I have never seen a new strategic plan that didn't have a set of five-year hockey stick financial projections attached to it, and I include every single strategic plan that I have put together over the last twenty-five years!

The successful business leader will drill into the details around the financial projections to understand why these assumptions will drive the rapid rise up the hockey-stick financial performance. If the business and the strategic process does not have a rational answer or, heaven forbid, the previous plan saw this very same hockey stick last year and the year before that, smart owners will fire the CEO; but what about if you are the CEO and the shareholder?

You need to learn a pragmatic and rational approach to forecasting future revenues. What's Plan B if the resource revenue assumption fails to materialise? Take a growth projection and shrink it; does the plan still hold together? What does it mean regarding increased market share and is that realistic to gain? Will we have enough cash and is the capital investment justified? Should we phase investment more slowly into overhead and prove the plan before we race ahead?

This is a tension between two rights: i) invest gradually, stage the growth, and protect the business; or ii) invest quickly, see rapid growth, and take advantage of the opportunity. Only the robustness of the plan can dictate which is the correct choice.

Build a realistic financial model with appropriate sensitivities

Action -

- Construct two financial models to show the rapid vs. staged growth options.
- Take a sensitivity pen to the key numbers, revenue growth rate, gross margin performance, overhead investment and see how the plan stacks up.
- Model where the cash comes from and when it's needed.
- Throw in a couple of *what ifs* in case something goes wrong.

And there we have it, we have built a brand-new world strategic plan. Let's recap those key action points before we move onto Step 3: Building a High-Performance Culture.

Identify your unique point of competitive positioning and define VPA

Action -

- Articulate exactly what your brand and business proposition is going to be.
- Describe your vision, purpose and ambition, clearly.
- Establish what your customer couldn't get anywhere else if you didn't exist.
- Set it in the context of the market you plan to attack.
- Define your point of competitive differentiation.
- Understand that it's probably not going to be a radical strategy but be ready to identify how you will win.
- Be clear about what you are going to do differently.

Focus on the areas that you have the power to control

Action -

- identify the big picture trends that could impact your sector in the medium term.
- Be clear about what the core competencies of your organisation are.
- Articulate how you will change the value chain to adapt to the shift in strategic intent.
- Detail where you want to play and how you will win.
- Understand the impact of time on your plan.

Define the resource requirement for the new plan

Action -

- Start to align resource requirement—physical, human, and capital— with strategic intent.
- Map where the cash will come from and when you will need it.
- Understand what core competencies the strategy will need and spot the gaps.
- What are the critical success factors?
- Build in technology as an enabler.
- Be clear who your star climbers are, you will need them at some point.
- Plan for when it goes wrong and have a contingency.

Build a realistic financial model with appropriate sensitivities

Action -

- Construct two financial models to show the rapid vs. staged growth options.
- Take a sensitivity pen to the key numbers, revenue growth rate, gross margin performance, overhead investment and see how the plan stacks up.
- Model where the cash comes from and when it's needed.
- Throw in a couple of *what ifs* in case something goes wrong.

In some ways, although building the plan is the most important part of the five-step programme, it is also the easiest. We are all adept these days at PowerPoint strategy, producing glitzy sophisticated business plan presentations that guide the audience through a gilded and serene world to the promised land. Make sure that you stay grounded while you go through the process— grounded in reality and grounded in truth. It's much less painful in the long run.

In Step Three: we will now equip you with a toolkit to start the process of building a high-performance culture, sharpening the focus of your organisation's activities to deliver performance improvement, and progressing on your journey to success and excellence.

In Britain, we have many areas where we lead the world; thinking, development, and progress. I could go all misty eyed and reminisce back to the days of the Empire and start quoting screeds about the obvious ones. George Stephenson and his steam train the Rocket, Alexander Graham Bell and the first telephone, Joseph Swan and the light bulb, John Logie Baird and the television, Charles Babbage and the programmable computer, etc. But we can also point to more recent examples where Britain has achieved incredible success and led the world. What about Tim Berners-Lee and www., or John Shepherd-Barron and the ATM machine, or James Dyson and the bagless vacuum cleaner?

We could be controversial and also include in this list of things Britain has given the world, like North America. Back in 1775, it was a British colony. The colonists, who were all British subjects, argued with the UK government about taxation without representation (some things in life never change!) and eventually fought the War of Independence. Victory in 1783 gave them independence, and overnight they became Americans but up until that point, in their formative years, the colonists were British subjects and therefore by any degree of reasoning, the USA at its inception was a British gift to the world.

We could also be magnanimous and include nearly every major sport the world now plays. OK, I accept that baseball (clearly derived from rounders) and American football (clearly derived from rugby) by said British colonists in the paragraph above might be tenuous and that we can hardly lay claim to the Olympics. But the global power sports, football, rugby, cricket, tennis, golf, motor racing, (did you know that the first prearranged match race of two self-powered road vehicles over a prescribed route occurred at 4:30 a.m. on 30 August 1867, between Ashton under Lyme and Old Trafford a distance of eight miles, between Isaac Watt Boulton and a Mr Schmidt of Manchester?) were all given to the world by the Brits, even if we no longer dominate performance in any of them!

And it would be remiss of me not to highlight Sir Isaac Newton again here, a man who led the thinking that now forms the base of most modern physics.

If we look outside of the inventions arena, there are numerous recent examples where our thinking and performance is still at the sharp end of global progress. Think modern video gaming, Rockstar North, and Grand Theft Auto; think architecture and some of the amazing global buildings that Zaha Hadid and Sir Norman Foster have designed. Think scientific research and the DNA work being undertaken across the UK to better understand the genetic process through which cancer spreads; think Dave Brailsford and Team Sky who have positioned British Cycling at the forefront of the global sport.

Whether it is in the arena of invention, sport, intellectual reasoning, or the pursuit of progress and higher standards, all these great people and businesses share one fundamental attribute: in the way best suited to their strategic intent, they create a culture that delivers high performance as a systematic matter of course. It is the very DNA of their being and thinking, and there are such clear lessons for us to learn as we approach the task of improving the performance of our organisations.

And at this point I will throw one more onto the table; the world's leading aerobatic display flying team......the **Red Arrows**.

If you ever get the chance to hear Jas Hawker speak, I wholly recommend you take it. Hawker is a former leader of the Red Arrows, Red 1 and his motivational speaking takes the audience on an engaging journey to understand how the Red Arrows maintain their position as the pre-eminent aerobatic flying display team the world has ever seen. Drawing clear parallels with the commercial world, Justin outlines the planning behind air displays, the purpose of debriefing and the need for continuous improvement. With a remarkable Red Arrows film, he also demonstrates the critical importance of clear communication and shows how organisational excellence is both achieved and maintained.

His is, without a doubt, the most impactful presenter I have experienced and he made me rethink much of what, and how, I build a high-performance culture. I see four key component parts: i) building a team around you to make it happen; ii) benchmark yourself against how good you can be; iii) unlock the potential of your business-critical people; iv) focus your best people on the big opportunities.

Over the last twenty-five years, this change in my thinking has shaped Steps 3 and 5 of my programme. At this point it is important to differentiate between your close-knit team and the high-performance culture that makes the new world plan happen across the organisation; and the culture of buy-in and motivation across the broader organisation. For sure, you need both, and nothing should ever stop you driving towards having both. In Step 5, we look at creating the latter, but in this step, it is all about creating a close-knit Team 1. It is about you having your lieutenants around you. It is about you knowing that the guys in the trenches next to you will hurt just as much if it doesn't happen. It is about how to make a business successful, and how to create a culture that delivers sustainable success.

It is clear that so much revolves around the people that make it happen— not just the leader but also the board and the business-critical people, the ones who you would miss if they walked out the front door. I have grown to call them Team 1. They are your team; the team you surround yourself with; the ones you trust explicitly; the people who you are confident enough about to put into their hands, your life, your future, your dreams, your summit.

To build a tight, cohesive, totally aligned Team 1, I believe you need to work on creating the following: you need a common sense of ambition and a really clear view of what your legacy as a team will be. It has to extend beyond just numbers; it has to have a real *why* in it. It has to be relevant to the values and the personal drivers of your Team 1.

Then you start to put a team together that demonstrates three clear attributes. I call them, i) **desire**: how badly do you want it? ii) **belief**: how strong is the sense that it will be achieved? and iii) **commitment**: how important is it beyond anything else in the world? These three attributes deliver *trust* throughout the team and become the barrier for protecting performance and spirit when it gets tough out there.

Nowhere is this more visible than in big climbing expeditions. At altitude, you have a Team 1. Sometimes it's only two of you. The difference is you know that at some point on the climb you are likely to have not only put your dreams of a summit into their hands but that there will be a high likelihood of you actually putting your life in their hands; that is real *trust*.

Step 3 of our programme will now equip you with a toolkit to start the process of building a high-performance culture, sharpening the focus of your organisation's activities to deliver performance improvement, and progressing on your journey to success and excellence.

In his brilliant book, *Legacy: What the All Blacks Can Teach Us About the Business of Life,* author James Kerr walks the reader through his time observing the team and its preparation for the Rugby World Cup in 2010.

He starts by talking about the *haka*; the ritualised challenge thrown down by one group of warriors to another. I guess we have all seen it on TV before a big game, and no matter how many times you see it, it always makes the spine tingle.

Opposing teams face the haka in different ways. Some try to ignore it, others advance on it, most stand shoulder to shoulder to face it out. Whatever their outward response, inwardly the opposition know they are standing before more than a collection of fifteen individual players. They are facing a culture, an identity, an ethos, a belief system - and a collective passion and purpose beyond anything they have faced before. Often by the time the haka has reached its crescendo the opposition have already lost, for rugby, like business and most of life, is played out in the mind

-James Kerr

The All Blacks are the most successful rugby team of all time. They have been called the most successful sports team in any code ever. In the professional era, they have a win rate of 86%. So how do the All Blacks do it? What is the secret of their success? Where does their competitive advantage come from? What can we learn from it?

Owen Eastwood, a lawyer who includes the All Blacks team as a client, uses an equation: Performance = Capability + Behaviour. Leaders design and create an environment, and the brilliant leaders create a culture that drives the behaviours they need to be successful. The All Blacks have utilised this better than anyone. The haka is one key component part of the culture that shapes the All Blacks.

My thinking and experience extend beyond this. I believe very strongly that there are two additional parts to the success equation. There is another saying in professional sport and business, which concludes that *luck* is what happens when preparation meets opportunity; but you already know my view on luck, 'Nah, it doesn't exist' so I have an equation that has driven the success in all of the companies I have been fortunate to lead.

A high-performance culture and sustained success is achieved when: *preparation + opportunity* align with *capability + behaviour.*

For me, I like to break down the component parts in the following way:

- **Preparation** - In All Blacks terms, this is how they prepare for a big game or a tournament; it's the tactics, the plan, the level of fitness, the playing system, and the knowledge of the opposition. All are hugely important. In business, I see this as the attributes and actions we discussed in Step One: Where are we right now? What do the numbers tell us? What has stopped us being successful so far? Is the organisation aligned?

- **Opportunity** - In All Blacks terms, it is about taking advantage of the way the game pans out; dictating rather than being shaped by the opposition. In business, the opportunity is wholly centred on the strategic choices you made in Step Two: do something new, take advantage of emerging possibilities, build on what you do well, be clear about propositions and differentiation.

- **Capability** - In All Blacks terms this is about the talent and playing standard of the team and the component parts. In business, this is about getting the right people around you, building a strong and committed Team 1, identifying the business-critical people you need, and ensuring that skill set and competence are aligned with strategic intent.

- **Behaviours** - In All Blacks terms, Kerr very strongly makes the point that this is the factor that sets the team apart and drives the win ratio. The culture that surrounds the All Blacks drives behaviour to an elevated level that no other team can match. In business, here I see little difference. To build a truly high-performance culture as we see in every case study throughout the book, to make *excellence* the norm, you need to attach behaviour to a consistent ethos. I will keep referring to it as 'the way we do stuff round here'.

Ethos is a word derived from the Greek word for character; it articulates a distinctive set of characteristics, values, attitudes, culture, principles, behaviours, and spirit of either an organisation, a team, or an individual. I have always used it as a reference point to describe to people that 'it's the way we do stuff round here' and in his book *Legacy*, James Kerr uses ethos in a very similar way to describe why the All Blacks have a competitive advantage over other national rugby teams.

In my experience, it's easy to encapsulate ethos into a poster or a set of buzzwords but it's infinitely harder to use the ethos you define to shape the very essence of Team 1; to make your behaviours and values come to life, and to turn words into actions and to make the team principles define the way you think and act consistently. If you can find the way to make your ethos come alive, your Team 1 will become a powerful force in much the same way as the All Blacks have an 86% win rate.

Kerr also contends that the All Blacks' competitive advantage is their ability to manage their culture and central narrative by attaching the players' meaning to a higher purpose. It is the identity of the team that matters, and not so much what they do but what they stand for; who they are and why they exist.

To become an All Black means a stewardship of a cultural legacy. Your role is to 'leave the jersey in a better place than you found it'. The humility, expectation, and responsibility this brings, lifts their game. It makes them the best in the world.

He tells a very powerful story following a New Zealand vs. Wales game in Dunedin 2010. After the game, which the All Blacks won 42-7, they go through a debrief session in a similar way to the Red Arrows. It's about what we can do better. it's direct and unsparing. Everyone gets a chance to speak and they focus on the areas that need work. *'The challenge is to improve, to always get better, even when you are the best. Especially when you are the best.'* But this isn't the most powerful part because after the debrief, Kerr tells how two players— one twice an international player of the year - pick up two long-handled brooms and start sweeping the changing room, brushing mud, and rubbish into the corner. The All Blacks look after themselves, doing it properly, so no one else has to.

This is powerful stuff. It's called Sweeping the Sheds and it's what leads to a deeply ingrained culture; it lives values, it creates a legacy, it builds the ultimate Team 1; the most powerful Team 1 in the world.

Contrast this with the constant media focus we see so regularly playing out around the overpaid, over-indulged, over-glamorised stars of the English Premier League. The last twenty years has seen so much money flow into the upper echelon of English football. Wages and transfer fees have spiralled to dizzying heights. And yet, in this time, we have seen a deterioration of playing standards, performances on the international or European stages, and no sense of loyalty or commitment. The average EPL footballer is now a fully card-carrying mercenary, available to the highest bidder, ready to move at the drop of a 'bigger wedge' and happy to pull on a new coloured strip and kiss the badge for the fans.

There is no sense of culture, of legacy, of there being a Team 1 with values or ethos. Reflect on Chelsea during the 2015/16 season. They were the previous year's champions and, by any evaluation, the team of the season. They started the new season as though they had never played together before. They had a manager who seemed intent on alienating as many players as he could as quickly as he could (not to mention his backroom staff), a captain who was quite happy to announce publicly that he had not been offered a new deal, which appeared to conflict with the club's view and with the owners who pulled the trigger on the manager less than half-way through the season, even though he was the most successful manager in the club's history...Wow! Hardly the stuff that the All Blacks are made of!

I wonder when the last time was that a Chelsea player swept the dressing room after a game.

What is interesting, though, is that this new style of football team— be it Chelsea or in an even more extreme example Manchester City who regularly buy up the 'supposedly' most talented and definitely the most expensive players— does not deliver sustained and consistent success. Similarly, at Real Madrid, the strategy of buying a team of *Galacticos* has delivered three titles in the last twelve years, in contrast to the eight that Barcelona have won with their focus on building the Barcelona way and bringing the nucleus of the team through the academy. It will be interesting to see how Manchester City adapt in season 16/17 to Pep Guardiola their new manager, who helped to create the Barcelona ethos and who, if we believe the press about him, has no time for overpaid prima donnas.

The dynasty that Sir Alex Ferguson built at Manchester United (Man Utd) was also built on values and ethos, albeit in a slightly dictatorial way and perhaps with an 'old school' management style. Nonetheless, though, it had a grounding in reality, with a nucleus of home-grown talent, which was ruled mercilessly by Sir Alex. How many games did Man Utd win in injury time because the sense of being Team 1 just didn't give up? That hunger to win for the team was enough to get the late winner. Isn't it also interesting that so many of the Man Utd team from the golden Ferguson years have gone on to be successful in management themselves?

So don't underestimate the power of Team 1 and the part it will play in delivering you sustained success.

Now, for sure, there is a stack of other things that make the All Blacks, Barcelona, and Man Utd some of the world's most successful sports teams. My suggestion is to read Legacy and it will provide you with all the insight you need. In much the same way, you will look at your business and conclude that executing all the component parts of your strategic and annual operating plan will make you a raging success. It's not just about culture, behaviours, and ethos.

But I contend that without these three things deeply embedded into Team 1, your ability to bring alive the actions necessary to deliver the systematic focus on constant improvement will be sub-optimal.

If the team do not understand the *why*, how do you create a culture where they are energised to take on responsibility, make decisions, implement changes, and stay true to the very vision which is the key to your success?

Now, let's talk about Team 1 and how you get to it. Using either the Red Arrows or the All Blacks as a living, breathing example, it is quite simple; they are close-knit teams that are clear in their construct. In a broader shaped, possibly multi-site organisation, how can you find your version?

I like to think of it as follows: either you make Team 1 you and leave it at that (but I don't recommend it!), or you make Team 1 you and the board, and your senior executives; or you make Team 1 you, the board and your business-critical people; or you go big time and make Team 1 the entire organisation or site—challenging, but possible.

My preferred option has always been to have my Team 1 as the nucleus of senior executives around me. The team that help to define strategy and then implement the plan; usually it has been my board, so five to six other directors, and they are always an integral part of defining ethos, values, and culture.

You need to decide what gives you the best chance of success. There is no absolute right answer, and it can change through time. But always remember it's about, *desire, belief, commitment,* and *trust.* It's about the adoption of culture, vision, ethos, and values. It's about a total buy-in to 'the way we do stuff round here,' and it's an absolute commitment to your equivalent of leaving the jersey in a better place than you found it.

Who is in your Team 1 and are they aware?

Action -

- Be clear about the composition of Team 1.
- Make sure that everyone knows they are part of Team 1.
- Define ethos, values, and behaviours that Team 1 will subscribe to.

- Articulate the culture and purpose you want and how it translates into a higher meaning for your key players.
- What is the legacy you are trying to leave? Does everyone get it?
- Can you demonstrate your equivalent of 'sweeping the sheds'?
- What is the sense check to make sure it's working?

Every young boy wants to be a
Red Arrow Pilot

I am sure we have all seen them perform at some point in time. It is the most amazing display you will ever see, often in dubious weather conditions but always right at the pinnacle of high performance. If you can tear yourself away from the routines they fly and reflect for a brief minute on what they are actually doing, it makes our process of running a successful business seem remarkably mundane.

These pilots fly at speeds of up to 600 miles an hour, coping with G-forces of 7G and above. They can fly as low as 100ft off the ground and regularly fly in a nine-plane formation at 400mph with each plane only six feet from the next one. Everything is calculated by the naked eye; no autopilot and no mechanical aids; everything is down to the pilots and the team.

Every year three pilots leave the Red Arrows squad, and from the pool of very best talent, the team leaders identify three new ones. The process ensures a continuity of performance and no reliance on individuals but puts enormous pressure on the new team to relearn every offseason. The recruitment process to bring in the right talent is challenging and exhaustive but in this team *trust* is everything. They recruit on the basis of flying talent, but they have one other key motivator, how badly does the new pilot desire to improve? How strong is the belief they can make it? How deep is the commitment to getting there? Without alignment on these three things, there is no *trust* in *Team*.

The squadron motto on their crest is *Éclat*, meaning excellence and perhaps this is the reason that the Red Arrows are the best in the world: because they don't measure themselves by anyone else's progress. Ask them who they compete against, and they only have one answer, ourselves. Their sole focus is on being the best they can be, challenging themselves always to be better, to deliver more, to raise the bar.

This mindset is an attribute that we see in all high-performance teams and one which you need to establish and perpetuate across your organisation. We saw with the All Blacks, the desire to get better even when you are the best; especially when you are the best. It is the same at Team Sky, which is what we look at on the following pages.

A crucial stage in the Team 1 formation process is the definition of what 'great' looks like. A crucial part in the Team 1 performing stage is the constant appraisal of how to make 'great' better. How to reach the sustained performance level between exceptional and phenomenal, which Steve Peters always drills into Team Sky. Be prepared to spend time on both. It will be a hugely valuable investment.

The whole Red Arrow's raison d'etre is to showcase excellence. The team ethic is a desire for excellence, and that's what they represent. They feel it is important to not just show off trickery in aeroplanes at shows, but that they also show professionalism and the standards achievable through hard work.

The Red Arrows have a legendary debriefing session after every flight where they calmly and openly reference their mistakes to the other pilots, a process which is kicked off by Red 1, the team leader, or Boss as everyone seems to call him. They use this as a part of the drive for continuous improvement— marginal gains as Dave Brailsford always references. The Red Arrows prefer to think of it as doing the simple things excellently.

In business, I like to title this as your **critical success factors**; what are the five or six things, which if executed with ruthless efficiency, will make the difference between success and failure? How clearly are they articulated around the business? How closely and how often are they evaluated for delivery? We can all list a hundred things we need to do when running a business or a team. As part of your new process, discipline yourself to list the five focus areas for success and then keep a spotlight on them.

At the Red Arrows, pilots will routinely talk about flying in their box— a mythical space around the plane from which their teammates know they will not exit. This gives the other pilots confidence that if they too can fly in their box, then 400mph at 6ft apart is not actually that risky!

But at this point, they also recognise the contribution of the support team— the 'the blues' as they are known— who prepare the planes to the nth degree to ensure that the performance standards of the equipment match the performance level of the pilots— demonstrating that excellence has to permeate the entire organisation.

So the next time you sit in a board meeting and look around the table at the people with you, I urge you to ask yourself a question: would I trust this person to fly 6ft from me at 400mph? Do I believe this person wants to be the best as badly as I do? Does this person believe in what we are looking to build here as much as I do? Is their commitment to making it the reality as deep and strong as mine? When you can answer yes to all four questions, you are on your way to a high-performance culture.

Team Sky and the Tour de France

In June 2008, Dave Brailsford, the performance director of British Cycling, was talking at a Sports Journalists' Association lunch in London. Buoyed by the success of British riders in the UCI World Championships and feeling very optimistic about the prospects for gold medals at the forthcoming Beijing Olympics, Brailsford revealed publicly his vision for a British-sponsored, British-run professional team to compete at the Tour de France, the other road classics, and to become a force in professional road cycling.

The announcement of the team had three specific objectives: create the first British winner of the Tour de France within five years; inspire people of all ages and abilities to get on their bikes, through the team's positive profile, attitude and success; add further support to competitive cycling in Great Britain.

At the beginning of the following year, satellite broadcaster BSkyB announced the formation of Team Sky, to be managed by Brailsford and the first six riders signed to the team are all British: Geraint Thomas, Steve Cummings, Chris Froome, Russell Downing, Ian Stannard, and Peter Kennaugh. Brailsford continued to build the infrastructure around the team during 2009 with one outstanding question always on the lips of journalists, who would be the team leader?

At the 2009 TDF, Bradley Wiggins arrived in France riding for the Garmin-Slipstream team. He had lost 6kgs in weight during training and felt in great shape for the Tour. Typically known as Wiggo to everyone, at that year's tour he became 'Twiggo.' He clearly fancied his chances of doing well and perhaps deliver the best finish by a British rider at the TDF.

Wiggins was born in Ghent in 1980 and was the son of an Australian professional cyclist and an English mother. Two years after Bradley was born, his father left the family, and mother and son moved back to England, living in a flat in Kilburn. He fell in love with cycling watching the Barcelona Olympics in 1992 and seeing Chris Boardman win Britain's first cycling gold medal in the individual pursuit. Later that year, at age twelve, he entered his first race, The West London Challenge 92 and his cycling career was born.

Over the next few years, Wiggins progressed rapidly through the junior ranks, winning his first national title at the age of sixteen and following up the next year with five titles. In 1998, he went to the World Junior Championships in Cuba and returned with the Individual Pursuit gold medal. Two years later he made the Olympic team for Sydney and with partner Rob Hales won his first Olympic medal, Bronze, in the Team Pursuit.

Wiggins continued to develop his career both on and off the track, winning titles and medals across the world, becoming a three-time Olympics gold medallist, and winning numerous World Championship events. By 2009, when he arrived in France he was considered a threat to Lance Armstrong— the favourite to win that year's Tour. A strong showing over the three-week period saw Wiggins finish fourth, missing out on a first podium finish for a British rider in Tour history but nonetheless a strong signal of capability. By December 2009, the feverish press speculation over Wiggins joining Team Sky came to an end when the three-time Olympic champion's move from Team Garmin-Slipstream was confirmed. Wiggins became the 25th Team Sky rider, would be the undisputed team leader, and moved for a reputed transfer fee of over £1m.

So Brailsford had his British team, a strong title sponsor, and a British team leader who had demonstrated the capability to perform well at the TDF. He was aligning his resource— human, physical and financial— behind his strategic intent. The first two years of the team showed progress towards the stated ambition, winning tour stages in 2011 and performing well at other Classique races, but it was the background work that the team was doing which was showing the important progress.

Brailsford had long held the view that winning the Tour would be the culmination of a series of 'marginal gains' across a broad range of process and activity. He recruited to the team a strong technical support network, which focused on specific areas, including an Aussie, Tim Kerrison.

Kerrison is a former rower who made his reputation in Australia coaching the women's sprint swimming team. Despite no previous cycling experience, he joined Team Sky in 2010 with the remit to rewrite the team's training schedules. He started by analysing the critical success factors of a Tour winner, quickly reaching the conclusion that the rider who generates the most power, for the longest duration, while weighing as little as possible, and slipping efficiently through the air, usually wins the race. From this point, every turn of a Team Sky riders pedal was recorded by a power meter, analysed using performance software, and then benchmarked against Kerrison's 'power curve' models.

In 2011, Wiggins's training was assessed against a template for a Tour/Olympic double. The power curve gaps between these two lines on a graph - where Wiggins was and where he needed to be - were where Team Sky directed what Kerrison describes as 'coaching interventions.' His main one was in addressing Wiggins' weakness in the mountains by focusing on altitude training, weight control, and power output. When he won gold in Beijing, Wiggins weighed 80+kgs, by the time he arrived at the 2012 tour, he was 68kgs.

Extended training camps at altitude throughout the winter were introduced; reverse periodization, which turned the idea of a gradual build-up to the Tour on its head; less racing, and more training during the season. Using pre-tour races as a preparation for the main objective, refining strategy, physical conditioning, or tactical approach.

Team Sky would also use the people-management principles devised by Steve Peters, the 'mechanic of the mind', author of the book *The Chimp Paradox* and a psychiatrist who had worked at Rampton Secure Hospital. He focused on the riders, enhancing their understanding of how the mind works, teaching them how to manage their emotions, behaviours, and thinking. Removing negative thoughts and keeping the rider fixed on success, Peters would drill into the team... 'You need to consistently be somewhere between exceptional and phenomenal.'

The marginal gains didn't stop there. The team's dietitian, Nigel Mitchell, was a constant presence at races, monitoring every gramme the riders ate, preparing the special meals that the team consumed, all made in a mobile kitchen, specified by the chef himself. The story about Team Sky carrying all the riders' own mattresses around Europe in a van and installing them in the hotel each night has become legendary.

More training staff were hired, so that, uniquely in professional cycling, Sky's riders would benefit from one-to-one training on a constant basis. 'You can see from this team how much you can get by investing relatively small amounts in coaching,' Kerrison told the press while Brailsford backed this up with his comment.

'It's better to have a £900,000 rider with a £100,000 personal coach than to have a £1m rider with no coach. The gains are disproportionate.'

On bike technology, the team reached an exclusive agreement with Pinarello to design and develop new models with specific performance attributes, changing the shape of the bike's tubing. Clothing was addressed next with Rapha developing a completely new performance range for the Team to enhance the aerodynamic gain. Other areas were looked at, riders' pillows travelled with them, everyone used hand gel to limit the risk of infection, every aspect of a rider's life was analysed to identify the 1% gain.

The result...in 2012, Bradley Wiggins and Team Sky won the Tour de France.

Two years ahead of his plan, Brailsford had achieved the goal he'd set out for Team Sky. After ninety-eight years, Britain had a TDF winner and a TDF-winning race team. A second Sky rider, Chris Froome, also finished on the podium to complete the domination of that year's tour for the team.

What happened next tells you everything about Brailsford and his approach. Wiggins went to London and won Gold in the Olympic Time Trial to complete his fantastic summer. Not content with winning the 2012 Tour and achieving his strategic objective, Brailsford took the team back to their base and immediately started to plan for 2013. What could they make better? Where was the next set of marginal gains? Which riders had more potential? Thus, the new plan was built.

The result...in 2013, Chris Froome and Team Sky won the Tour de France.

So now it's time for me to be a little controversial and express my view on Sir Dave Brailsford and his 'marginal gains' approach to achieving the team's objectives.

If you break down exactly what Brailsford has achieved and how, you see less about the pure generation of marginal gains and way more about the pursuit of excellence. For sure, in some areas, the benefit of a change in resource or process may have resulted in a gain that was marginal, but across the piece, the majority of changes that Team Sky implemented were material and delivered significant performance benefits.

Take the training and physical conditioning routine introduced by Kerrison. The gain here was not marginal. The gain here was probably the single biggest contributor to winning two tours and the identification of the **key critical success factor**:

'the rider who generates the most power, for the longest duration, while weighing as little as possible, and slipping efficiently through the air, usually wins the race.'

Then there was the process change to measure and analyse every single pedal revolution of every single Team Sky rider to deliver first Wiggins and then Froome as that rider.

So my contention is that Brailsford created a cycling centre of excellence, and he just used the phrase 'marginal gains' as a hook to hang everything he was doing on. He went through his plan and aligned his resource accordingly— human resource: get the best riders (remember he wanted a British winner) so he secured first Wiggins and then Froome; support them with the best backroom staff, Kerrison, Peters, individual coaches for each rider. He acquired the best physical resource: better bikes, clothing, food, living conditions during races, training venues, all critical success factors in a tour victory; and, finally, he secured financial resource: using the sponsorship from BSkyB to ensure that his team had the best and leading cutting edge technology and investment.

He then created a culture within which, isolated success was not enough. Winning the tour in 2012 achieved the objective, but it wasn't enough. In climbing terms, he asked the question, how can we go higher? Where is the next summit? What does success really look like?

After a disappointing tour in 2014, with Froome crashing out of the race by day six, Brailsford tells the story of driving through France with his Team 1 in the car. They shut down all communication tools and started the process of building a *new* new world plan.

Brailsford described the 2014 race as 'a horrible experience. You've got to go through those horrific moments if you really want to get to big results. If you just want the middle ground, do all right, it's all OK - that's not what we want.' The defeat led to a realisation amongst the senior management that Sky had become set in their ways after three successful years. 'We drove six hours to Paris, phones off, and I grilled the management all the way: 'What are we going to do to turn this round? This isn't good enough. This isn't what we are all about. This isn't excellent.' And excellence is what we are supposed to be all about.'

The core group around Brailsford consist of the head of performance operations, Rod Ellingworth, the physiologist, Tim Kerrison, and Carsten Jeppesen, who is the team's backroom principal, and it was amongst the four of them that the discussions took place.

'We all looked very hard,' Brailsford said. 'We'd been becoming pretty aligned over the last six years working together. If you gave us a problem we'd come back with the same answer, we had lost the cognitive diversity we had as a group. Before when I would say something, they would say 'bollocks', we'd argue a lot, there would be tension but we'd come up with some good ideas, constantly pushing forward.'

Brailsford has a reputation as a manager who is demanding to work with, who shakes up his colleagues, and who likes creative tension. The return to that was key, he felt. 'It's comfortable, everyone getting on but it wasn't excellent. So if we want to change this, we're going to have to rock this boat, as uncomfortable as this is. It's a pain in the arse to do it. It's going to be stressful, it's not going to be pleasant but ultimately you have to rock it from side to side, bring new people in who will question everything, ask why we are doing this, take us forward.'

Bear in mind that these words are coming from the business leader who has just won two TDFs following a stellar career at British cycling. His star rider crashed out of the Tour. How easy would it have been for Brailsford to kid himself that everything would be OK next year? Reset the budget for this year, put the rose-coloured glasses on, do all the things we went through in Step One and yet, no, he builds a new plan, challenges the team to get better, benchmark themselves against how good they could be, redefine what excellent looks like.

The result...in 2015, Chris Froome won his second Tour de France. In 2016, Froome won his third TDF and Team Sky won their fourth in five years.

Now ask yourself how comfortable it feels in your business. Where are the challenging conversations about performance, people, and results? When was the last time you really looked at how good you could be and what does excellent look like? Now is the time to kick the process off and really drill into the critical success factors that will create the performance culture that delivers sustainable success.

Desire, Belief and Commitment = Excellence

Action -

- Test the desire to create excellence in everything you do.
- Identify the five or six critical success factors for your business and focus on process delivery.

- Ensure that your recruitment process is robust and brings you the best of the best.
- Is there a formal debrief process to evaluate delivery?
- Have you got the right team and can you learn from the red arrows rotation?
- Do you benchmark yourself annually against how good you could be?
- Are the performance standards transparent in the business?
- Have you got enough desire, belief and commitment where it matters?

If I had a pound for every time I have heard or read a business leader tell someone else that his people are his biggest asset, I would by now be lying in the garden of a sunny Caribbean villa, sipping gently on a smooth rum-based cocktail, and contemplating whether my golf game is actually in good enough shape to think about joining the Seniors Tour in America.

It is nonsense...total nonsense, and the sooner we dispel the myth the better.

There have been any number of surveys done over the last thirty years and all tell us the same thing. Modern thinking on employee engagement articulates that any organisation can identify a split of employees into three camps:

Engaged employees work with enthusiasm and passion; they want to know the desired expectations for their role so they can meet and exceed them. They perform at consistently high levels. They want to use their talents and strengths at work every day. They have an intuitive connection to their company and will constantly endeavour to drive innovation and move their organisation forward. They get the *why*.

Not engaged employees aren't necessarily negative or positive about their company. They see work as a source of income and work because they have to. They have little or no proactive interest in work, often being labelled 'nine-to-fivers'. They often have an arms-length attitude towards their job, their employer, and their co-workers, but they generally do what is asked of them and don't cause any trouble.

Disengaged employees are 'Consistently Against Virtually Everything.' Not only are they unhappy at work, they are always taking the opportunity to make sure that their co-workers see and realise it. They become a source of negative energy across an organisation, constantly undermining what engaged workers are striving to achieve.

Typically, the split in the average business will be Engaged 30/35%, Not Engaged 50/55%, and Actively Disengaged 15/20%.

So let's head back to the previous two sections and ask ourselves some questions. How would you feel flying a Red Arrow jet at 400mph, 6ft from a co-worker and you had a pretty strong feeling that they were 'not engaged' in making the Red Arrows the centre of flying excellence? Or how many World Cups and how long would the 86% win rate last for the All Blacks if every time they crossed the white line, 70% of the team were not engaged or were actively disengaged in doing the haka?

Your biggest asset is not your people; it's the small nucleus of your team who are actively engaged with your vision for the business. Who understand the higher purpose that their roles build up to. Who come to work with you because it provides them with the opportunity to realise their personal goals and ambitions. It becomes a hugely integral part of making them what they are and, for sure, they need the money but never lose sight of how far down the list that comes when they make their decision criteria about where to work. These form the nucleus of your business-critical people; cherish them.

So you have a number of tasks to undertake in creating a high-performance culture. Firstly, you need to be very clear about the competencies and capabilities that you need to deliver constant improvement and functional excellence. You need to identify the attitude and behaviours required to consistently execute the plan, and you need to have total clarity on the gaps you have. Then you need to map this to your human resource and decide how you fix what you see. There are two fundamental ways: replace or repair.

In Step Five of our programme, we focus on the repair part. We call it Motivate, Engage, and Mobilise to create Momentum, and we will walk you through ways that you can invest in the organisation and its people to transition your engaged ratio to a higher level.

By far, the greatest untapped source of wealth and potential in any organisation is all those people who have chosen on that particular day not to bring their energy and motivation to work. The 'not engaged' part of the workforce who leave their passion and their initiative on the bedside table every morning and coast through the day. These capabilities, energy, motivation, passion, and initiative are the attributes we need most from our employees. These capabilities that are impossibly difficult to command but are easy to inspire.

Jack Welch and the GE phenomena

General Electric was formed in 1892 following a merger between Thomas Edison's East Newark-based Edison Lighting Company and the Thomson-Houston Electric Company of Lynn, Massachusetts, run by Charles Goffin. In 1896, General Electric was one of the original twelve companies listed on the newly formed Dow Jones Industrial Average and after 120 years, it is the only one of the original companies still listed on the Dow index.

It has been a pioneer industrial conglomerate for over a hundred years, constantly at the forefront of innovation and sector development across America, and increasingly across the world. In the early years, it was clearly at the cutting edge of both electrics and lighting, but can also lay claim to starting RCA in 1919, the Radio Corporation of America, which we still know today as the home of artists such as Justin Timberlake, Alicia Keys, and Britney Spears and although no longer part of GE, was the home of the world's first phonograph in 1929.

GE will also lay claim to making the world's first public broadcast on their 1.5sq inch and rather snappily named W2AXD TV. In 1927, Ernst Alexanderson beamed pictures to the homes of four senior GE executives and the world of home TV was in motion.

Over the life of the group, GE has been actively involved in many sectors: aviation, power generation, computing, consumer finance, plastics, and healthcare. It has consistently ranked as one of the leading Dow Jones companies. Even today it is ranked at number eight on the Fortune 500.

In 1981, the business had global revenues of $28b. It made $1.6b in net income, employed 400,000 people, and had a market cap of $13b...it had also just appointed the youngest chairman and CEO in its history, Jack Welch.

Welch joined General Electric in 1960. He worked as a junior chemical engineer earning a paltry salary of $10,500. Within a year he had decided to leave, frustrated by a combination of money and bureaucracy. He was persuaded to stay and went on to build a stellar career, rising quickly through the ranks at GE. By 1968 at the age of thirty-three, he was VP and head of the Plastics Division. Further senior roles followed. In 1973, Welch was named the head of strategic planning for GE and he held that position until 1979, which involved him now working from the corporate headquarters, exposing him to many of the 'big fish' he would one day be amongst. Not long after his promotion to head of strategic planning, Welch was named senior vice president and head of the Consumer Products and Services Division in 1977, a position he held until 1979 when he became the vice chairman of GE.

In 1981, he replaced Reginald H. Jones as chairman and CEO of GE. He was 46 years old.

Now, a plethora of books have been written about Jack Welch, and what he achieved at GE and the purpose of using him as a case study here is not to add to them. Indeed, he has written a number himself, which clearly articulate how and why he achieved what he did. By 1988, revenue had increased to $50b with net income doubling to $3.5b, but GE now had a workforce of fewer than 300,000. Welch was driving a strategy of only remaining in sectors where GE could be the global number one or two brand. If they couldn't, the business, no matter how profitable, was disposed of.

What kind of zebra are we?

There are some very disparate views on Jack Welch and his style. Nicknamed Neutron Jack for his ability to eliminate employees while leaving buildings intact, he had an uncompromising style. He worked to eradicate perceived inefficiency by trimming inventories and dismantling the bureaucracy that had almost led him to leave GE in the past. He closed factories, reduced payrolls and cut lacklustre units. But at the same time, he pioneered a policy of informality at the workplace, allowing all employees to have a small business experience at a large corporation.

He also introduced the world to 'Rank and Yank' or perhaps as it's more elegantly called now, the Jack Welch 20/70/10 style of employee differentiation.

Welch believed that in an organisation, employees could be broken down into a performance differentiation. He believed 20% were the stars and A-players, 70% are average but dependable, and the bottom 10% need to be gracefully released from the company.

This, or a similar, approach to ranking employees was used by many other organisations at the time: Motorola, IBM, Enron (!), Dow Chemicals, Ford, Microsoft, and GSK all had their own versions of employee differentiation. Most, but not all, were oriented to providing significant rewards to the top tier and to removing the bottom tier from the organisation. Welch was quoted on numerous occasions saying that his approach to the all-stars resulted in them being treated differently. He would say:

> *'Make them feel loved, hug them, give them cash, give them rewards in the soul and wallet. Do everything for them.'*

His approach to the middle 70%, was to show them what they need to do to get into the top 20%. For the bottom 10%, he believed that you should tell them why they should move on. That it should be done as part of performance reviews and be concluded within a year.

Welch always said this method was much better than false kindness where employees aren't told they aren't good, and then they take a termination or layoff as a surprise. Welch advocated that you should not create an expectation, but rather create candour. Every year the GE Operating Company CEOs had to force rank their teams and remove the bottom 10%...regardless.

Welch believed that with training and investment, with time and opportunity, that visibility of reward could transition people from the 70% average into the 20% all-star category and continue the lifeblood of the organisation. He also believed that knowing there was a bottom 10% and what would happen if you drifted down there, was a motivation to the lower echelon of the average 70% to keep them focused.

So when asked, what would you say is your company's greatest asset? Your products? Your technology? Your brand? Jack Welch would answer that it is the same for every business: your team. But then he would qualify the statement. 'This whole game of business revolves around one thing,' he would say. '**You build the best team, you win.**'

After his tenure as CEO much has been written about the 20/70/10 style of differentiation and there are as many sceptics as there are followers. But the one thing that no one can take issue with is that, when Welch retired from GE in 2001, he had built the market cap to more than $500 billion, GE employed 340,000 people, revenue topped $110 billion, and net income was over $10 billion.

The numbers never lie…!

While the ratios don't correlate exactly, there is a strong alignment between the research done into employee engagement and the JW forced ranking system. For me, I never used the JW system; I found it too direct for an SME business, but I did adopt the principles of his approach to ranking people and employees.

So in all my businesses, I would have Team 1, the guys around me that I trusted and knew had my back. Then I would have my equivalent of the JW all-stars; I liked to call them my Business-Critical People. These were the top 20/30% of employees who made the difference; who got it done; who were passionate and committed to the vision and the purpose. They were the ones who made the product launch successful, who delivered outstanding customer service, who championed change and made it happen, who didn't need direction but consistently demanded responsibility. They were the ones who produced exceptional work on time, and who exuded energy and motivation. The ones who you just knew if you allowed them to walk out the front door and not come back, the business would be a weaker place.

So I had my own version of showering them with rewards and hugs!

The BCP got the majority of my attention. I invested more time in them than in anyone. If I walked the building, it was the edge of their desk I would sit on to chew the fat. If I went for lunch in the canteen, it would be at their table I would sit. If I wanted to know something it would be them I would go to. I would always support them with training, with investment, with the opportunity to travel to new markets, with the chance to test products and go do the stuff that we were passionate about. If a promotion or pay rise was mooted, I always found a way to make it work or at the very least would sit down with them personally to help them understand where I would get them to career-wise and what was at the end of the journey for them.

When we discussed strategy, I made sure that the BCP had a voice. I would regularly conduct briefings for them, update them on the performance and progress of the business, and keep them involved in what next. If they were in our international markets I would make a point of travelling and following the same pattern with the offices and markets when I got there.

Around the business, these people became known as my chosen ones, but I never worried about that. As far as I was concerned, this was the team who would make our vision and our ambition happen, therefore other people (and it was usually the disengaged) could think what they wanted.

For the middle 70%, I was always watching them and looking for the next all-star— the next one with the potential to become a BCP. When I spotted it, I would start to over-invest to make sure I was right. If I was, then quickly they transitioned into the all-star category and would benefit accordingly. For the balance of the 'averages', I would always make sure they didn't feel neglected, would get the briefing, and the updates but not the special close attention. I invested yes...but not to the detriment of the Business-Critical People.

Next, there was the need to address the final group— the disengaged part of the workforce— and never make the mistake of thinking that these are the guys who just do the routine run of the mill jobs. In my experience, these people are right across your organisation, from the Board down; highly prevalent in management and a cancer that will eat away at all the good you do elsewhere in our five step programme.

You need to identify the disengaged and any not engaged who you believe will be too hard to transition very quickly. Now is the time to get rid of them; no questions, no discussion, no arguments. Move them out of the business in an appropriate way. Treat them with dignity and respect but don't dodge the issue. It doesn't really matter how much the short-term cost is, you have no capacity to carry passengers. There is no place in a high-performance culture for people who don't care or for people who don't sort it out.

> *if it looks like a duck, if it walks like a duck*
> *and if it quacks like a duck*
> *it will forever be a duck...!*

I had a little black book of names always with me; a list of the disengaged who if they left I just knew the business would be a better place. I never quite got to the GE process of removing 10% every year— that felt onerous to me. But I would always be working on where I could strengthen and how to do it.

Interestingly, a bit like Welch, my experience here is two-fold: i) you never act quickly enough - it's a fact! I cannot think of one occasion when I knew I had a duck and I gave it a chance to become an all-star and it changed...never, never, never....but I can name numerous instances where I took action and then wished I had done it sooner; and ii) if you do it properly and have managed the appraisal process effectively, then almost without exception the employee is relieved once you reach a conclusion with them.

Make Business-Critical People your biggest asset

Action -

- Map your human resource base.
- Identify the business-critical people and start investing in them straight away.
- Define the competencies and capabilities you need to execute the plan and decide where your gaps are.
- Evaluate E/NE/DE against your behaviours.
- Take action immediately to get rid of the ducks.

It's an immutable law of life, and therefore of business, that time does not expand to fit the work created. The only thing no one in the history of the world has learned to make more of is time. Without managing your time, anything you do, no matter the size or importance, can cause you to fall victim to Parkinson's Law: Work expands to take up the time available to finish it.

At the same time, when we are leading organisations we always see beyond the current and face a huge wall full of opportunity. It's what makes us the entrepreneurs we are, that constant pursuit of what's next, the drive and ambition to be better, bigger, with more customers, more products, more revenue and more markets.

The successful warrior
is the average man with laser focus
-Bruce Lee

And yet somewhere deep inside we know and understand that neither we nor our people have an inexhaustible supply of time and energy and if we delve deep enough into our psyche we will find the corner of our mind that tells us the businesses and brands we aspire most to be are single-sector limited product companies.

Which brings me to Steve Jobs, Apple...and a broken promise!

Now, when I started to write this book I promised myself two things: firstly, I would do my best to keep it succinct and interesting and the sort of book that you could dip into depending what issue you were wrestling with at the time; and secondly, that I would NOT under ANY circumstance reference either Steve Jobs or Apple.

You decide if I have achieved my first promise. I am about to break my second one.

I get incredibly frustrated listening to speakers and article writers talk about Apple and what Steve Jobs did. Almost every case study will revolve around their success and will be held up as the way to do it. For sure he was an amazing guy and created an amazing business that still leads the world. For sure we can all learn stuff from the Apple way and for sure I am sitting here today writing this on a new MacBook Pro. But the reality is Jobs did what he did, at a time when he could do it and from a starting point that allowed him to do it. For those of us running businesses right now, our starting point is different and the time is certainly different.

But I want to call out one thing that Jobs did because I believe it is a business principle that we can all follow regardless of our starting point or situation.

When he returned to Apple in 1997, he took a company with 350 products and reduced them to ten products in a two-year period. Why? So he could put the A-team on each product. Jobs was as proud of what Apple chose not to do as he was of what Apple did. Current Apple CEO Tim Cook explains that one of the core principles Steve Jobs instilled in the company was the need to stay focused on doing only what you do best. 'It's easy to add ... it's hard to stay focused,' he said. 'And so the hardest decisions we make are all the things not to work on.'

'That's been one of my mantras - focus and simplicity. Simple can be harder than complex: you have to work hard to get your thinking clean to make it simple. But it's worth it in the end, because once you get there you can move mountains'
-Steve Jobs

I call it the Art of Laser Focus...focus on your focus...pay all your attention, using your best people, on your biggest opportunity. Don't get side-tracked. Don't chase moonbeams. Don't allow distractions. Really understand if what you are looking at is truly core to your strategic plan. Will it help deliver your goals? Will it bring the summit closer? If the answer is yes then throw every resource you have at making it successful. If the answer is no or even worse maybe...DON'T DO IT!

The Innovation Kitchen

Now I have to admit that visiting a Nike head office is somewhat akin to acting in an edition of the Stepford Wives. Either the Beavertown powerhouse brand operates a previously unidentified indoctrination of all new employees or a combination of the company vision espoused by founders Phil Knight and Bill Bowerman in 1968 and the culture perpetuated by current CEO Mark Parker is sufficient to ensure that almost every Nike employee gets *why* and can verbatim articulate the company's goals and purpose.

My guess is the answer probably lies somewhere between the two.

What is interesting about Nike though is the way it has used innovation to maintain its position as the leading global brand in performance sport. The process through which they have delivered over fifty years a compelling stream of patented and groundbreaking innovations is a closely guarded secret. A visit to the Nike HQ in Portland allows you to glimpse the famous Nike Innovation Kitchen but sadly never to cross the threshold. Folklore dictates that the majority of Nike employees have never been permitted to enter and that it's a 'chosen few' who get to spend their time playing about in the kitchen.

The Nike model is not massively dissimilar to Apple and in fact, Tim Cook, the current CEO of Apple, is still on the Board of Nike. Get your best people working on your biggest opportunities, then let the rest of the company work out how to commercialise the innovation. But the system works. A stream of innovations in footwear (Air/Air Max/Zoom/Flyknit) textiles (dry-fit, dry-tech) technology (Nike+, fuelband) or equipment (golf balls) has consistently kept the brand at the forefront of its sector and has built a company with global revenues in excess of $20 billion.

They invest heavily in R+D, putting all their best people into the kitchen and then giving them sufficient resource to deliver an innovation pipeline that becomes the lifeblood of the business. For sure, globally, $30 T-shirts are probably the biggest product revenue driver, but if you look at a category like Nike Air, Air Jordan, and Air Max, which have become global brands in their own right, the constant drive to innovate the technology has created a lasting technology franchise that is as desirable today as it was when launched in the mid-80s.

This type of approach has also delivered amazing success for a British company, Dyson, the innovators of bag-less vacuum cleaners. Much has been written over the years about how James Dyson eventually succeeded in bringing his vision to build a bag-less vacuum cleaner to the global market; how it took him five years and 5,127 prototypes to perfect the product; how he used the income from selling his first product to the Japanese to build the DC01, the original product that launched the brand and the business.

These days, the Dyson brand has global sales of £1.7 billion and makes an operating profit of £448m, all built around global sales of vacuum cleaners, lighting, fans, and hand dryers. They still have their central R+D function in the UK and use the Dyson Foundation to ensure there is a talented stream of young engineers and designers available to maintain the ethos of the business. Refine-Improve-Refine-Improve...as James Dyson articulates it:

'Our mission is simple; we solve the problems others seem to ignore'

At Berghaus, we approached innovation and positioning in a similar way to both Nike and Dyson although I dare say with a slightly lower level of investment! When I took over as CEO, I was surprised and possibly a little shocked to see that we had so few patents, very little innovation coming through, no discernible pipeline of cutting edge products, and we didn't really have a structured process to deliver the product innovation we needed to compete in the global market.

We very quickly identified that to compete we needed to invest; align resource behind strategic intent. We established our own version of the innovation kitchen and we called it MtnHaus.

We took a number of our most talented product and design people and literally locked them into a room. We took away their day jobs and involvement in the broader business and provided them with the opportunity to focus on delivering a pipeline of innovation. They were able to go out and talk to our performance athlete base, to listen to the product requirements they had that Berghaus was not meeting. We had an amazing stable of athletes—some of the best high altitude climbers in the world; Leo Houlding, an incredible Big Wall climber who was driving the most extreme expedition adventures in the world; endurance runners, adventure racing teams, downhill bike racers, etc. The feedback was so valuable.

The MtnHaus team also spent time with the consumer base, getting the feedback from loyal and serious users, travelling to our global markets to see how consumer need for the product was different when climate and terrain changed. They were able to focus on building relationships with component suppliers and specialist manufacturers to ensure that product construction was using the most cutting edge technology. We invested in a full capability sample room in our HQ in Sunderland, allowing the team to take their ideas from initial concept to nearly finished sample without fear of exposure to the competitor set.

And more than anything, we gave the team time. It was probably the hardest investment but the most valuable. There was no pressure to hurry the new innovations to market. The focus was to get them right, make them world class, make sure they work, be clear where the value add to the user was...then we launch.

Over the next ten years, Berghaus, through the MtnHaus team, started to lead the world in product innovation. It took eighteen months to bring the first products to market, but once the pipeline was in motion, it built up very quickly. Soon we had so many innovative products— the world's lightest Gore-Tex jacket, the first European brand to use water resistant down, the first brand to make a vented waterproof jacket, the first hybrid down and synthetic insulation clothing, body-mapped construction to protect core organs, and a hyperlight clothing range. The Berghaus name started to win multiple awards at trade and consumer shows; consumers began to recognise the best products that money could buy.

The key message here is to build into your culture a ruthless laser focus on delivery of your biggest opportunities and get your business-critical people onto it. Be clear about what you are choosing NOT to do and how this is allowing you to focus valuable resource on creating *excellence*.

When it comes to anything important in life, more is never better. Better is better. And best is even better than that. In terms of everything that matters - love, passion, focus, attention - the more things you have, the thinner you're spread and the less you'll come to value them.

Laser Focus all your resource on the biggest opportunities

Action -

- Be clear about where your big opportunities lie.
- Get your best people onto them exclusively.
- Make laser focus a cornerstone of culture.
- Articulate what you are choosing NOT to do.
- Are you investing enough in your differentiation?
- Where does your innovation come from and what is your equivalent of the innovation kitchen?
- Don't rest until you can confidently say, 'We are the best we can be'.

So that's Step 3 finished. We have our tools and techniques outlined to create a high-performance culture. Let's recap on the key action points before we move onto Leadership the Brand

Who is in your Team 1 and are they aware?

Action -

- Be clear about the composition of Team 1.
- Make sure that everyone knows they are part of Team 1.
- Define ethos, values, and behaviours that Team 1 will subscribe to.
- Articulate the culture and purpose you want and how it translates into a higher meaning for your key players.
- What is the legacy you are trying to leave? Does everyone get it?
- Can you demonstrate your equivalent of 'sweeping the sheds'?
- What is the sense check to make sure it's working?

Desire, Belief and Commitment = Excellence

Action -

- Test the desire to create excellence in everything you do.
- Identify the five or six critical success factors for your business and focus on process delivery.
- Ensure that your recruitment process is robust and brings you the best of the best.
- Is there a formal debrief process to evaluate delivery?
- Have you got the right team and can you learn from the red arrows rotation?
- Do you benchmark yourself annually against how good you could be?
- Are the performance standards transparent in the business?

- Have you got enough desire, belief and commitment where it matters?

Make Business-Critical People your biggest asset

Action -

- Map your human resource base.
- Identify the business-critical people and start investing in them straight away.
- Define the competencies and capabilities you need to execute the plan and decide where your gaps are.
- Evaluate E/NE/DE against your behaviours.
- Take action immediately to get rid of the ducks.

Laser Focus all your resource on the biggest opportunities

Action -

- Be clear about where your big opportunities lie.
- Get your best people onto them exclusively.
- Make laser focus a cornerstone of culture.
- Articulate what you are choosing NOT to do.
- Are you investing enough in your differentiation?
- Where does your innovation come from and what is your equivalent of the innovation kitchen?
- Don't rest until you can confidently say, 'We are the best we can be'.

Businesses often miss the intrinsic link between strategy and execution. Setting strategy is theoretical. It's a clean and analytical process of collecting and processing data, generating insights, and identifying actions and steps forward to the brave new world. The output is a smooth narrative in a professional-looking document made up of Venn diagrams, 2?2 matrices, and high-level plans of attack.

Then the trouble starts. Execution happens in the real world. The clean and elegant logic of the plan gets dirty as external, and internal forces compete. Priorities clash, decisions stall, and communication breaks down; timelines get blown. In climbing parlance, the weather changes;

a massive storm blows in. It's never a question of *if* these problems will happen; it's a question of when and to what degree.

Managing these challenges takes street smart, muscle, and a supremely high-performance culture.

In Step Four: we will now identify some key actions you can take to enhance your leadership brand and impact on your organisation; how you use your personality and influence to deliver results, to engage, and to inspire your followers.

Over the last thirty years, there have probably been more books, articles, and words written about leadership than any other facet of the evolving business world. There are more definitions of leadership styles than you can shake a stick at, there are more examples of iconic leaders than you can ever remember, and there are any number of leadership development courses thrust in front of us every day. We are constantly challenged to be a better leader, to be a different leader, to be a new world leader, to be the leader our business and our people need us to be.

And yet, given the huge pressure demands that we live our lives under as CEOs or business leaders, how much time are we able to dedicate to developing ourselves? To develop and refine our leadership style? To create space in our busy working lives when we can stop and think: what kind of leader am I trying to be?

'What is my Leadership Brand?' because that's what it should be, a brand.

We live in a world now where virtually everything is branded in one form or another and our customers— in this case, your people and the organisation— make their decision whether to buy— in this case, to engage, to follow, to be inspired— based almost entirely on how they see your leadership brand.

At its core, the basic premise of business leadership will never change. There will always be a need for individuals who can motivate, inspire, and encourage their teams to work together towards common goals. In trying to differentiate between leadership and management, I like the way that John Kotter, professor of leadership at Harvard Business School describes it: 'Leadership is about aligning people to the vision, that means buy-in and communication, motivation and inspiration.'

'If the world is not changing and you are on top, then management is essential, but more leadership is not,' says Kotter. 'Leadership is always about change: it's not about mobilising people to do what they've always done well to continue to do it well.'

'Management is a set of processes that keep an organisation functioning. They make it work today - they make it hit this quarter's numbers. The processes are about planning, budgeting, staffing, clarifying jobs, measuring performance, and problem-solving when results did not go to plan.'

I think it was Peter Drucker who said, 'You lead people, you manage things.'

When people are asked to define the ideal leader, most will respond using traditional command or authoritative attribute-based language. Character traits such as intelligence, toughness, decisiveness, determination, and vision are the qualities traditionally associated with leadership. Such skills and attributes are necessary but insufficient qualities for the leader. Often left off the list are softer, more personal qualities—but they are also essential. These days, followers will be looking for you to demonstrate humility, compassion, values, and strong communication skills alongside the technical capability. Studies indicate that emotional intelligence may now be the single biggest key attribute that distinguishes outstanding leaders from those who are merely adequate.

I challenge you to think this through in your organisation; Leadership is not what you do—it's what others do in response to you. If no one shows up at your march, then you're not a leader, and if people do decide to jump on board because you've inspired them, then it means that you have created a bond of trust within the company, which is essential especially if the business is rapidly changing and needs people to believe in its higher purpose.

They buy into your *leadership brand*, and that is a very, very powerful weapon to have.

Daniel Goleman, in another paper on leadership for Harvard Business Review, *Leadership that Gets Results*, offers the following view; drawing on the research of more than 3,000 executives, Goleman explores which precise leadership behaviours yield positive results. He outlines six distinct leadership styles, each one springing from different components of emotional intelligence. Each style has a different effect on the working atmosphere of a company, division, or team, and, in turn, on its financial performance. The methods and styles, by name and brief description alone, will resonate with anyone who leads, is led, or, as is the case with most of us, does both.

- **Coercive** leaders demand immediate compliance.
- **Authoritative** leaders mobilise people towards a vision.
- **Affiliative** leaders create emotional bonds and harmony.
- **Democratic** leaders build consensus through participation.
- **Pacesetting** leaders expect excellence and self-direction.
- **Coaching** leaders develop people for the future.

Results demonstrate that leaders who get the best from their teams don't rely on just one leadership style; they use most of the styles in any given week. Goleman maintains that with practice, leaders can switch amongst the six leadership styles to produce powerful results, thus turning the art of leadership into a science.

Step 4 of our programme will now identify some key actions you can take to enhance your **leadership brand** and impact on your organisation, how you use your personality and influence to deliver results, to engage, and to inspire your followers.

At school I played six different sports at representative level, going on to turn professional at golf and revelling in the harsh testosterone world of competition. My ego and my need to win and be the best was fuelled by regularly stepping into the Gladiators' amphitheatre. I grew up as a typical alpha male, coming down the final stretch in a big golf tournament. You instinctively knew that the first one to blink was the loser. Playing each different sport was only ever about winning, about crushing those in front of you to demonstrate your power, your control, and your ability to master the universe.

And this alpha-male personality was what drove me to be successful in business. Leaving golf in 1987, I started to build a career in the commercial world. Initially, roles with retailers House of Fraser and Beales led me to become an MD before I was thirty. It was a small business— twenty-odd people— distributing other companies' branded products but I was the top dog. I was the guy who called the shots. I was the big kahuna, and it felt good.

Over the next ten years, I developed my career, almost entirely in MD or CEO roles. Leading organisations to deliver powerful results, I am proud of the fact that I have left every business I have run in better shape than when I started, that I have developed hundreds of people over the years, and watched many go on to be leaders of businesses in their own right.

In 2003, I joined a business called the Pentland Group, an organisation privately owned by the Rubin family, run by Stephen Rubin the father and serial entrepreneur and Andy Rubin, the Harvard-educated CEO; a powerful combination. The family had made their initial fortune investing into Reebok, a small sport-shoe brand in 1984; buying a 55% stake for $75,000 days before the brand was about to go out of business. In 1991, when Reebok, by this time a global power brand, was floated on the NYSE the family shareholding was worth $775m.

They now own a portfolio of premium-branded businesses in the sport, leisure, and fashion sector and are one of the foremost global brand management companies. I joined them to run Berghaus the iconic British outdoor brand and business the family had owned for over ten years. My brief was to globalise the brand and take advantage of the explosion of demand and participation in all types of outdoor activity as the stresses of modern life caused the mass population to reconnect with nature and the great outdoors.

But I had a bit of a problem. First, I had never led a global business before; second, I had never led such a talented team before, and third, I had never been in a job where I didn't have all the answers before. And yet no one in the organisation was aware of these three minor issues!

Everyone was patiently waiting to see what my *leadership brand* would look like. It was scary, which to an Alpha Male is not a great place to be. Fortunately, I stumbled onto a solution, more by luck than by judgment. Some of the other executives in the Pentland Group had completed a course at Ashridge Business School— *Leading Strategy and Change*— and the following spring I enrolled in the course.

Nowadays, I always call it a life-defining moment. Maybe that sounds a bit *Hollywoodesque*, but nonetheless, it had an amazing, incredible impact on my life and my leadership style.

The strategy piece was extraordinarily useful. With no qualifications of any sort, as a CEO I did what I did intuitively, worked on instinct, and had been fortunate that in every role, I had been successful. At Berghaus that would not have been enough and the course equipped me with a framework to use as we globalised the brand. To be honest, it didn't change so much, but it gave me a structure that I had lacked.

> **'Oh, what a great gift we would have**
> **if we could only see ourselves as others see us.'**
> *-Robert Burns*

The huge message was about *leading*, and *change* and I learned more over the next five months than I had learned in a lifetime. They start by scaring you to death. They do what I began calling **Holding a Mirror up to Your Face**, which is a painful and revealing process that shows you with incredible clarity just how others see you. And trust me…it's very scary!

You begin to understand the powerful impact you and your leadership style has on the team around you as you lead and drive the change needed to deliver the shareholder ambition. They drill into the dark corners of your character, reveal the personality traits that you think make you successful but which all those around you find energetically and motivationally sapping.

They call you to task on how you communicate. Instinctively we deliver information in the style we like to receive information, paying scant attention whether that is right for our audience. At Ashridge we worked on a profiling tool called Myers-Briggs; this is a powerful tool for you to use with your Team 1. It will help you to better understand the characteristics and drivers of the team and will lead to much better clarity from discussions.

Let me give you an example. One of my senior execs (and a key component part of my Team 1) would often not say anything in a board discussion. He would listen but rarely contribute, and then regularly after the meeting would come into my office and express a valuable and powerful view on the topic of discussion. At times this was frustrating for me. I am an outgoing, and sometimes brash, extrovert. I like my board discussions to be structured, open, with good robust debate, have all the views on the table and then to reach a conclusion that the team then go on to action.

Often I would chide the exec to contribute in the meeting, but it never happened. Then after working with Myers-Briggs, I understood why. The exec was a strong introvert; he needed time to process and reflect on the differing views he was hearing. His ability to contribute came after he could think through the issue in a calm, quiet place not surrounded by seven very extrovert, very noisy, very loud colleagues all desperate to make sure that others heard their views on the subject.

Once I understood the personality profile I learned to adapt my style, not to try to adapt his, and consult his views on issues in a different way. Often we would discuss the topic before the board meeting. I was then able to get his strong contribution to the decision-making process.

There are lots of tools out there that can be used; Myers-Briggs is the one I have adopted, but my strong advice is to investigate them and find one that you and the team are comfortable with.

At Ashridge, they also check you on leading people and demonstrate that alpha-male leadership only works on a small minority of the population. They probe your motivations; is it all about your ego or is it truly about the greater good of the business and the higher purpose? They force you to develop a better understanding of how your team and the company see you. Using a technique called a 360 appraisal they get feedback from your team on what you are really like to work with. If you have never done one, try it but be prepared to learn stuff that will scare you. Also, be committed to change once you have a better understanding of the feedback, be committed to adapting your style to maximise the return from the people around you, <u>BUT</u> make sure you don't throw out any of the good stuff.

My favourite story of Ashridge, or perhaps I should describe it as my harshest lesson of Ashridge, involved the group I was in working on building a strategic plan for a case study business we had been looking at. It was the night before we were due to present to their Main Board, our strategic plan for their business, and to be honest, we were nowhere near ready, it was late, people were tired, we were getting nowhere, and there were too many disparate views. I decided that the session needed a bit more direction, a bit of leadership and I started to get more forceful in my views and more autocratic in driving towards a conclusion when in reality I had no right to be doing either!

After observing for a short while the lecturer running the session stepped in and asked me, 'Are you listening to the others in the group or are you just waiting for them to stop talking?'....BAM right between the eyes!

There and then I got a lesson that has stayed with me forever, did I react like that in my board meetings? Did I have a tolerance level, which once exceeded, would result in me directing the solutions to the board? Was there a point where I would stop listening and start ordering...so I went back to my team and asked them...YES, was the answer. That is exactly what you do.

If you have never done anything like this before then I unequivocally recommend you to sort something out right now. Take some time to explore your leadership style, invest some time and money in tools and techniques that enhance your capability. Over the last ten years, I have never stopped trying to learn, to build, and develop my leadership brand. I have studied global leadership at Harvard with some of the best teachers in the world. I have undergone one-to-one development work with a high-performance coach. I have taken a mentor who helps and advises me when I get stuck. I am always reading and absorbing lessons from the leaders of business, sport, and climbing who I respect and look up to.

All of the work in some small way has made me a better leader, someone people will follow, who can sell the vision and who inspires the extraordinary.

Be clear about how you should lead the organisation

Action -

- Define your leadership brand and map out how this is relevant to your organisation.
- Work out how you can invest in your leadership style.
- What do you need to adapt?
- Find a solution by holding a mirror up to your face.
- Understand the impact your style has on others.
- Start using a profiling and communication tool with your Team One.
- Complete a 360 assessment and map behaviour changes from the results.

It's a well-used adage, isn't it, that leopards don't change their spots. How often do you hear it said and isn't it nearly always describing a negative behavioural context? But the reality of modern leadership is that you need to find a balance; keep the spots, which are a powerful force, and use them sensibly while at the same time adapting the spots that have room and scope to grow and develop.

I used the leader descriptions from Golestone on the previous page, not necessarily because I see them as being the definitive answer but more as an illustration of the styles that are available to us. Coercive leaders demand immediate compliance. Authoritative leaders mobilise people towards a vision. Pacesetting leaders expect excellence and self-direction. Affiliative leaders create emotional bonds and harmony. Democratic leaders build consensus through participation. And Coaching leaders develop people for the future.

What intrigues me right now is how modern leadership thinking has drifted so sharply towards the new style of leadership where affiliative, democratic, and coaching leaders are seen as the current answer. We hear so much about the new theories surrounding transformational leadership; leadership that enhances motivation and morale by connecting the employee's sense of identity to a project and the collective identity of the organisation. We discussed it as a significant part of what makes the All Blacks such a shining example of Team 1.

Stephen Covey describes it as, 'The goal of transformational leadership is to 'transform' people and organisations in a literal sense - to change them in mind and heart; enlarge vision, insight, and understanding; clarify purposes; make behaviour congruent with beliefs, principles, or values; and bring about changes that are permanent, self-perpetuating, and momentum building.'

Current thinking has four major components of transformational leadership, which cover the full range of essential qualities a new world leader needs:

- **Individualised consideration**: the degree to which the leader attends to each follower's concerns and requirements, providing a supportive environment to unlock individual potential.

- **Intellectual stimulation**: the degree to which the leader challenges assumptions, takes risks, and seeks out the followers' ideas, allowing them to come up with their own solution even though it may be different to your own.

- **Inspirational motivation:** the degree to which the leader articulates a vision that is appealing and inspiring to followers, you communicate expectations and show optimism in reaching the goal.

- **Idealised influence**: the degree to which the leader provides a role model for high ethical behaviour, instils pride and gains respect and trust. They have a separate place for you in their heart. Your followers understand that you have great potential and determination, which will take them to higher levels.

And recent thinking seems to discard what may be considered to be old world leadership styles, coercive, authoritative and pacesetting as being inappropriate for the current day. The classic control and command style of leadership developed so strongly in the Forces or in the classic manufacturing industries seems to have no place in the modern world; often it is referred to as *Transactional* Leadership. The transactional leader works through creating clear structures, making it clear what is required of their subordinates, and the rewards that they get for following orders.

The transactional leader often uses *management by exception*, working on the principle that if something is operating to defined standards of performance, then it does not need attention. Exceeding expectations requires praise and reward, while some corrective action will be applied for performance below expectation.

In essence, *transformational leadership* has more of a 'selling' style. Transactional leadership, once the contract is in place, takes a 'telling' style.

A quick trawl through Google for examples of *transformational* Leaders throws up all kinds of names. The obvious are Nelson Mandela,

Mahatma Gandhi, George Washington, and Martin Luther King; the classic are Steve Jobs, Winston Churchill, Jack Welch; and the modern are Jeff Bezos and Mark Zuckerberg. When I then Googled examples of *transactional leaders* guess which was the most prevalent single name to come out? Sir Alan Sugar...closely followed by Donald Trump!

Now, my contention here is not that Zuckerberg is a role model and that Sugar is the devil incarnate. Alan Sugar has been running a successful business for more years than most, is a survivor through tough times and a changing world, has delivered his strategic objectives in his own style and successfully so. My contention is also that all of the leaders defined as transformational will have strong transactional tendencies when the time is right. Or will have an organisation that can adapt transactional process when required. Neither Nelson Mandela nor Steve Jobs was able to drive the change programmes they achieved so successfully without some semblance of a 'telling' style. Read *Long Walk to Freedom* or watch *Steve Jobs* the movie for validation.

Interestingly, I found as many references to Bill Gates or Vince Lombardi as transactional leaders as I did as transformational leaders; figure that one out!

My reflection on this keeps coming back to two things; you need to work out what style of leadership brand your organisation needs and then figure out how you **adapt your spots** to allow you to build and grow as a leader. By definition, there will be times when that is highly likely to include a mix of transformational and transactional as well as a combination of all six styles; just ensure you use them at the correct time.

Let me give you a couple of examples.

Sir Alex Ferguson - now a lecturer on leadership at Harvard Business School but formally one of the most successful football managers that the game has ever seen.

His record is legendary. In a career spanning almost forty years he won forty-nine trophies, with St Mirren, Aberdeen (including the European Cup Winners Cup, and the Super Cup) and of course Manchester United, where he captured thirteen Premier League titles, five FA Cups, four League Cups, ten Charity Shields, two Champion Leagues, one European Cup Winners Cup and three other global titles.

Any article you read about his time leading football teams and clubs is punctuated by classic old world style language. All are quotes directly from the man himself.

> *Never cede control.*
> *Change your team every three years.*
> *Make sure people know who is the boss.*
> *Set high standards and hold everyone to them.*
> *Be the first one in and the last to leave.*
> *I don't allow any player to be stronger than me.*
> *My personality has to be bigger than theirs (think Stam, Keane, Beckham and his plaster).*
> *Reprimand immediately people who fail to meet expectations.*
> *There is no other option to winning.*

He was the Boss, and everyone around United knew it. You didn't mess with him, or he would cut your legs off. He talks openly in his book *Leading* about how every four years he would work on reconstructing the team. This would mean a couple of 'stars' leaving the club to make way for either new signings or young players coming through. His message to the other players was explicit, no one at the club is bigger than me, and nobody is bigger than the club.

And yet in the archive section of *Leading*, Sir Alex has included a copy of a letter he sent to Eric Cantona in 1997 when Cantona retired from football. In it, he thanks Cantona for his time and wishes him all the best, but he concludes with the following paragraphs:

As I close this letter, I would like to hope that we will have a chat, a drink, or a meal together soon…the most important thing for me is to remind you how good a player you were for Manchester United and how grateful I am for the service you gave me. I will never forget that and I hope you won't either.

You are always welcome here and if you just pop in unexpectedly for a cup of tea, no fanfare, just for a chat as friends, that would mean more to me than anything. Eric, you know where I am if you need me and now that you are no longer one of my players, I hope you know you now have me as a friend. Good luck and God bless.

Sir Alex Ferguson demonstrating his capacity as an affiliative Leader!

In a modern world, Ferguson delivered outstanding results using almost entirely old world styles. To many, this is the anathema of modern leadership but in reality, Alex Ferguson was able to find his perfect style and deliver sustained success. In 2012/13, his last season, he won the title with a less than average squad, dragging them over the line with his unique brand of leadership and despite spending hundreds of millions since, the club are no longer the force they once were.

We shall see where Senor Mourinho now takes the club over the next few seasons!

Through the glory years, Ferguson bullied, cajoled, abrased and drove his team to title after title. His ability to secure 'Fergie time', the extra bit of additional injury time that referees added to escape the wrath of the Man Utd manager on the sidelines while United went in search of a winning goal is legendary. 100% transactional.

But balance this with his approach to managing a team of super-talented youngsters. He was a father figure to so many and the individualised consideration he gave will for sure have created the environment within which they flourished. Giggs, Beckham, Scholes, Butt, the Nevilles, Rooney, Ferdinand, Ronaldo all enjoyed long and successful careers because Ferguson recognised the need to be a transformational leader.

Adapt your spots…

What about Vince Lombardi, coach of the mighty Green Bay Packers and globally recognised as the forefather of great sporting team leaders. Lombardi started his coaching career at West Point in 1949, learning under the direction of the great Red Blaik, head football coach at the United States Military Academy, for eighteen seasons.

It was not until he reached West Point and combined his spiritual discipline with Blaik's military discipline that his coaching persona began to take its mature form. Blaik's emphasis on execution coupled with Lombardi's own desire for simplicity would become a trademark of his coaching. He developed a reputation for being a tireless workaholic; a trait that helped Lombardi land a position as assistant coach in the NFL for the New York Giants.

During his five years with the Giants. Lombardi led them to five winning seasons, culminating with the league championship in 1956. Lombardi became a hot commodity in the coaching arena, accepted the head coaching position and signed a five-year contract with the Green Bay Packers in January 1959.

Through the 1958 NFL season, the Packers, with five future Hall of Famers playing on the team finished with a record of 1-10-1. The worst in Packer history. The club and the players were dispirited, the Packer shareholders were disheartened, and the Green Bay community was enraged. The angst in Green Bay extended to the NFL as a whole, as the financial viability and the very existence of the Green Bay Packer franchise were in jeopardy.

From the outset, Lombardi established himself as a coach firmly in charge. His training camps were gruelling, and he demanded absolute dedication and effort from his players. His hard-edged style turned the Packers into the most envied and successful franchise in the 1960s, leading them to five NFL Championships in seven years, including victories in Super Bowl I and II, and reinforcing Lombardi's status as the greatest football coach in NFL history.

This is an extract from Vince Lombardi Jnr's book about his father, where he talks about his father and using many of his father's now immortal quotes, articulates how Lombardi Sr. approached creating a high-performance winning culture. It highlights a number of the leadership styles discussed and presents a very clear picture of Vince Lombardi's *leadership brand*. The book is called *What it takes to be #1.*

> *'Winning is not a sometime thing; it's an all the time thing. You don't win once in a while; you don't do things right once in a while; you do them right all of the time. Winning is a habit. Un-fortunately, so is losing.*

> *There is no room for second place. There is only one place in my game, and that's first place. I have finished second twice in my time at Green Bay, and I don't ever want to finish second again. There is a second-place bowl game, but it is a game for losers*

played by losers. It is and always has been an American zeal to be first in anything we do, and to win, and to win, and to win.

Every time a football player goes to ply his trade he's got to play from the ground up - from the soles of his feet right up to his head. Every inch of him has to play. Some guys play with their heads. That's O.K. You've got to be smart to be number one in any business. But more importantly, you've got to play with your heart, with every fibre of your body. If you're lucky enough to find a guy with a lot of head and a lot of heart, he's never going to come off the field second.

Running a football team is no different than running any other kind of organisation - an army, a political party or a business. The principles are the same. The object is to win - to beat the other guy. Maybe that sounds hard or cruel. I don't think it is.

I don't say these things because I believe in the 'brute' nature of men or that men must be brutalized to be combative. I believe in God, and I believe in human decency. But I firmly believe that any man's finest hour — his greatest fulfilment to all he holds dear — is that moment when he has worked his heart out in a good cause and lies exhausted on the field of battle - victorious.'

In the book, there are many more inspirational quotes and insights into becoming and staying number one. Lombardi is clearly practising the classic old school leadership styles. He is authoritative - mobilising the team towards a vision, he is coercive - demanding immediate compliance, and he is pacesetting - expecting excellence and self-direction.

The book also includes a lengthy passage where Lombardi Sr. articulates his approach to leadership:

'Men respond to leadership in a most remarkable way and once you have won his heart, he will follow you anywhere, leadership is based on a spiritual quality - the power to inspire, the power to inspire others to follow. Leadership rests not only upon ability, not only upon capacity - having the capacity to lead is not enough. The leader must be willing to use it. His leadership is then based on truth and character. There must be truth in the purpose and will power in the character. A leader must identify himself with the group, must back up the group, even at the risk of displeasing superiors. He must believe that the group wants from him a sense of approval. If this feeling prevails, production,

discipline, morale will be high, and in return, you can demand the cooperation to promote the goals of the community.'

In these two paragraphs, we get a real sense of the style of Lombardi's leadership brand. At a time when control and command were at their height and considering he shaped his style at West Point, Lombardi was years ahead of his day. He managed to combine the pacesetting style of leadership with an affiliative style, he was unbelievably demanding but at the same time, he understood the need to inspire a culture and translate a vision using powerful rhetoric. He always talked about the higher purpose and in the process became one of the greats of all time. He was a transformational leader in an old world.

Adapt your spots...

Be open to using different leadership styles at the right times

Action -

- Review your leadership style.
- How do you balance transformational with what got you here?
- How do you achieve the balance of old world/new world traits?
- What is your language to inspire your team with your vision?
- What are the no-compromise areas and does everybody understand them?
- What spots are going to get adapted?

When French novelist Jean-Baptiste Alphonse Karr wrote *'Plus ça change, plus c'est la même chose,'* he could have been directly referencing the challenge of driving change in a business or organisation. If you have successfully taken your organisation through the initial three steps of this book by now you will have reached two conclusions.

Firstly, 'that some things round here are going to have to change,' and also that 'we need a change plan to make it happen.'

Over the last forty-something years, in fact, probably dating back to 1979 and Michael Porters Five Forces, which changed the way business leaders viewed their companies, a huge industry has built up specifically aimed at helping businesses to effect change successfully. Amazon currently has 8,844 books on change management available if you have the time to read them all!

And yet despite the growth of this huge industry, despite the plethora of advice and education available to us, despite the knowledge that we need to engage with the hearts and minds of our workforce, and despite the conviction leaders demonstrate that we need to make this happen...two out of every three change initiatives are destined to fail.

The more things change, the more they stay the same

I am sure that we have all been through a Kubler-Ross **change curve** in our time. We know the set steps that transition us from where we are to wherever we aspire to get. It can be in business, in sport, in life, in relationships, in any area of our world, but at some point, we know we will need to change something.

The classic U-shape change curve has a series of stages. The start point is information, which is usually unexpected and triggers a rational response of shock and denial. This is often followed by an emotional reaction, anger, and frustration; why me? The bottom of the curve is depression, apathy, and detachment; 'I don't care'. The process of dialogue and bargaining kicks off when thoughts turn from concern for the past and potential loss, to concern for the future and potential gain; 'What's in it for me?' Experiment and understanding trigger acceptance and eventually a return to meaningful life. Somewhere between anger and depression, the whole process disappears under water at the bottom of the U-shape as you spin downhill and you reach the point where the entire process can disintegrate into a chaotic mess from which some extraction will be required.

> **'There is nothing more difficult to take in hand, more perilous to conduct, or more uncertain in its success, than to take the lead in the introduction of a new order of things.'**
> *Niccolo Machiavelli - The Prince (1532)*

Managing change is unbelievably difficult, but it's a vital part of the modern leader's role. I call it 'handling the difficult middle.' How do you steer your organisation through significant transformational change, without letting the change curve disappear under water half-way through the process? How do you keep motivation and belief high as you experience the toughest, darkest hours?

As an analogy, I always liken handling the difficult middle of a change programme to getting close to the summit of a really big, dangerous mountain. At altitude, your body requires more oxygen to handle the physical demands you make on it and yet at altitude there is less oxygen available. At 8,000ft there is 25% less oxygen available than at sea level and typically on a high-altitude climb, you will go above 20,000ft so it's not difficult to imagine just how challenging this becomes.

Eventually on a big climb, no matter how fit you are, there will come a stage where you feel like sitting down and not getting back up again. You will be tired from days or weeks of exertion, weak from lack of food, empty of energy from constantly forcing yourself to go on and go higher, exhausted from the cold and lack of sleep...each climber will find their own way to come out the other side of this darkest hour.

They will get up, they will drive on, and eventually, they will reach their summit.

Before initiating this change programme in your business you need to be very clear how you will manage the difficult middle, because one thing is certain, at some stage, your organisation will reach the point where it wants to sit down and not get up again! What process will you have in place and how will you motivate your people to get up and keep going?

For sure you need to incorporate the human side of the process—shaping culture, providing leadership, and changing behaviours— but you must also focus on having a clear and robust process plan. I like to think of this in a similar way to the six leadership styles. Part of the change process is transformational and part is transactional. The style and structure of your business will dictate how much weight you put towards each one, but you must be cognizant of optimising the balance.

The Boston Consulting Group developed a process for significant change management called DICE. It is weighted towards being a transactional process and requires an organisation to focus on four hard factors: i) **Duration** - how long will the project take, what are the milestones and how frequent will the review process be? ii) **Integrity** - who will drive and manage the change, how capable are the team, are your best people on the case? iii) **Commitment** - is there visibility from the senior leaders, have the team who will be affected by the change bought into the need for change, do people understand the *why*? iv) **Effort** - is there transparency on how hard it will be to make the change, do the team understand what is required, have the necessary steps been taken to backfill key roles?

This is one type of process but there are lots of different styles and processes you can follow and lots of consultancies out there who specialise in helping organisations to implement successful change programmes. Before you kick off, spend time with your Team 1 on mapping out your change process and make sure it has the required transactional and transformational elements.

LEGO - every child's favourite toy

Christmas morning used to be magical when you were a child. Whatever your eagerly anticipated toy was, it's likely that Lego would have been somewhere near the top of your list. You would wake up knowing that somewhere in the middle of all the presents would be boxes and boxes of new shiny Lego, which you could mix with your existing blocks and build loads of amazing creations. It's hard to accurately define the appeal of Lego. It appeals to young and old. It is enduring, colourful, and the appeal must lie partly in the fact that the potential to build something is almost infinite. A professor of mathematics recently calculated that there are more than 915m ways to combine six eight-stud Lego bricks...Wow!

But one thing is for sure, almost everyone reading this book will at some time in their life played with Lego!

Lego as we know it dates back nearly seventy years to when Danish carpenter Ole Kirk Christiansen made the first interlocking brick in 1949. He took the name from the first two letters of the Danish phrase *leg godt,* meaning 'play well'. Lego's knobbly plastic bricks and yellow figures are now known all over the world, and the business has to this day stayed in family ownership, based in Billund, Denmark, a village with a population of 10,000.

Like lots of companies, the path from its humble beginnings in 1949 to its global presence today, has been neither smooth nor trouble free. In the early 2000s, the Lego business and brand was in a parlous state. In the 1990s, the family and the executive board had made a series of strategic choices that time had revealed to be a mix of ill-advised and poorly executed diversifications.

The patent on the base Lego brick ran out in 1988 and resulted in a number of lower cost 'me-too' products flooding the market. Instead of staying true to the vision, purpose, and ambition and driving harder for core product differentiation as we saw Harley-Davidson achieve in Step Two, the board came to two clear conclusions: firstly, 'the Lego brick was going to die,' and secondly, 'the future is going to be digital'; both of which were clearly toxic conclusions.

Unlike John Lewis, who we also looked at in Step Two, the board of Lego then got two things very wrong. They built a new strategy almost solely around taking advantage of emerging possibilities but not focused on one and then failed to align resource behind strategic intent. The diversification strategy was centred on software, (Lego Moviemaker), lifestyle, (Lego kidswear), retail (Lego mono-brand stores), and theme parks (Legoland). Each move requiring a unique set of skills different from the core skill set and competencies within the Lego business and each requiring significant capital investment.

The result, by 2003, the company was in a pretty poor state; diversification had absorbed huge amounts of cash, the lack of focus on the core business had resulted in declining turnover, and the workforce was at best dispirited. The sharp and accelerating deterioration in the financial performance of the company forced the board to take a cold hard look at the reality of 'where are we now?'.

What kind of zebra are we...?

Jørgen Vig Knudstorp, then head of strategic development, was asked to undertake a review of the problems and produce a report for the shareholders. Knudstorp had joined the company from McKinsey & Company and was born within one hour of the main LEGO site. He had been a childhood fan of Lego and was keenly aware of the company's heritage.

His McKinsey training had taught him that 'fact finding is the first step to problem-solving' and would require a back-to-basics review and assessment. As we worked through in Step One, the first stage is facing reality— building the picture of exactly where you are right now— and this is what Knudstorp kicked off. Jack Welch CEO of General Electric once said, 'a good CEO must see things as they are, not as you wish them to be.'

What Knudstorp discovered was the harshest of reality and he realised that unless something changed dramatically, the business would not survive. He said at the time:

'We are on a burning platform, losing money with negative cash flow and a real risk of debt default which could lead to a break-up of the company.'

By 2004, the business had deteriorated further. As Jørgen Knudstorp explained to Diana Milne from Business Management Magazine, 'In 2003, we pretty much lost 30% of our turnover in one year. The decline continued in 2004 with another fall of 10%. So one year into the job, (Knudstorp became CEO in 2004), the company had lost 40% of its sales. We were producing record losses (2004 losses were $200m) and cash flows were negative. My job was how to stop the bleeding. We had to stabilise sales and cut costs dramatically to deal with the new reality of selling 40% less than we had done two years earlier. We had too much capacity, too much stock. It was sitting in the wrong countries. The retailers were very unhappy.'

Lego was lost in a strategic wilderness and disturbingly the management clearly didn't understand how far it was off track. The key stakeholders, customers, and employees were very clear about the problems but, there were no lines of communication to enable the key messages to get through to the top. What was getting said in the trenches was, unfortunately, staying in the trenches!

A complex management structure added little to cross-functional cohesion with twelve senior VPs overseeing six regions and operating in silos with little accountability. The alignment of resource was flawed. Everyone was working hard but in different directions. Critical success factors were not clear. Senior management was out of touch with stakeholders. It was a tug of war with all teams pulling in different directions.

Knudstorp continued to say, 'I think we found there were basically two fundamental challenges that grew out of this period - over stretching and over expansion. Focus had been lost on basic execution, simple things. We didn't know really what we produced on a weekly basis. There was a lack of transparency. We didn't know where we made money and where we lost money. It was obvious that the strategy was wrong but we didn't know what the right strategy would be, largely because the old one had looked like it was the right strategy.

So we actually, for the first two years of this new transformation of the company said, 'Look, we don't have a strategy. We just have an action plan', which is a detailed plan of back to basics, serving the retailers really well, making the products children really cared about, getting back to the core of what Lego had always been about, sort of a process of rediscovery.'

It's a really interesting point that he makes; *it was obvious the strategy was wrong, but we didn't know what the right strategy would be, largely because the old one had looked like it was the right strategy.* More often than not, this is what causes the difficult middle; you work through Steps One and Two of our programme, establish what kind of zebra you are, and make your strategic choices, but you don't always reach the right conclusions.

Then somewhere down the line, you need to reshape the strategy plan, (hopefully not as significantly as Lego needed to). It is not an exact science defining strategy. In lots of instances, it evolves and develops as you progress towards your vision and ambition. Like climbing a big mountain, you change the route as you climb, sometimes coming down to go back up, like Chris Bonington on the south-west face of Everest. The summit doesn't change but the plan to get there does.

Knudstorp developed a short-term action plan to ensure the business would survive. He focused on halting the sales decline, reducing debt, driving positive cash flow, exiting the ill-advised diversifications and focusing on core products and the core consumer. He also needed to sell non-core businesses, shed at least 1,000 jobs and dramatically slash the product offer. It was a classic turnaround role and required tight fiscal control and tight top-down management.

Nothing in the plan was radical or unique. It was a simple plan well executed.

1. Attack the cost base and rationalise (-30% SKU count) the product offer.

2. Slow the LEGO stores programme; shed the theme parks, and exit the computer business.

3. Restructure the product offer with better segmentation across Lego, Duplo, and Friends.

4. Introduce financial targets: line profitability, customer profitability, the ROS benchmark, FMC targets.

5. Get closer to the core consumer, putting the retailers first; focus on the supply chain; right product right place.

He created a clear vision for the future of the company, set a clear direction for LEGO, and fundamentally changed the way the company did business with major retailers, creating a clear command structure within the organisation with an emphasis on performance and profitability. Return to core values on product quality, the Lego legacy, and value for money proposition for end users and the retail customers.

Knudstorp also recognised the need for a higher purpose. Whilst the business needed to make money and grow, he believed Lego had a deeper purpose, *'to make a difference in children's lives by giving them wonderful play experiences and making this experience available to every child on the planet.'* Wow! If that isn't starting with *why*, I don't know what is.

'We'll spend a couple of years to stabilise the business and restore execution. We're going to spend three years restoring profitability and then eventually we're going to get back to organic growth.'

There was a process of open and honest communication put in place, Knudstorp regularly spoke to 500 senior and middle managers, appraising them of the change planned and of progress. Boards were put up across the business highlighting targets and progress; he regularly walked the floor talking to the broader nucleus of his workforce. The message was always the same: go back to basics, focus on the core business, improve margins, always stay close to the consumer.

This process of open communication and consistency of message, not just from Knudstorp but also from the rest of the executive team meant that he achieved strong buy-in to the new plan. People got where the company was going and why the change was needed, they recognised the burning platform and knew they needed to jump off or risk being burnt alive.

Interestingly Knudstorp clearly used a number of different leadership styles as he took the Lego business through this immense change programme. At times he was new world, democratic, and affiliative and yet at other times, he was old world, authoritative, and coercive. If you study his leadership style through the twelve years he has been CEO of Lego you will see all six of the Goldstone styles being utilised at different times and at different stages of the company's journey. A world class example of:

Adapt your spots

This is one of the best examples of taking a business through the *difficult middle*, driving a significant change programme, and disrupting the norm but for the better of the company; completely rebuilding the organisation's entire supply chain to ensure the right product in the right place at the right time. Knudstorp only achieved this because he recognised the need to, and how to, take the people with him.

In 2004, Lego was according to the Knudstorp review 'on a burning platform, losing money with negative cash flow and a real risk of debt default which could lead to a break-up of the company'. The company had reported losses of $228 million on sales of just over $1 billion in 2003 and a loss of $207 million on sales of $1.1 billion in 2004.

In 2013, the company achieved $4.5 billion of revenues and profits of $1.5 billion. Lego had replaced Hasbro to become the largest toy company in the world. Return on sales had increased to 33% and sales per employee had doubled.

The business is now hugely successful again, range developments into Star Wars and Harry Potter have reinforced the franchise with the consumer, these days over 50 billion Lego blocks are manufactured every year and every person on the planet on average owns ninety-two Lego blocks! In 2014, the brand, as ranked by the consultancy Brand Finance overtook Ferrari to become the world's most powerful brand.

Lego the Movie grossed $469m globally and was a cinema sensation. The company now has the Lego Foundation focused on understanding and developing children's learning. It has also introduced the Lego Ideas Platform where consumers and Lego devotees can send the company new product idea. If your idea goes into production you receive 1% of global revenue.

In 2015, the company achieved $5.3 billion in revenue and delivered profits of $1.8 billion...**the numbers never lie**.

Whether the BCG model is the right one for you, or whether you choose to draw more inspiration from the case studies written on the LEGO transformation, is a question for you and your senior team to answer. But my message is that you need to work out a process for making change happen successfully and it's a key part of your leadership brand. It is no longer enough to present the strategy PowerPoint and let others do it. The leader of the modern organisation needs to mobilise and motivate the team to deliver fast and successful organisational change or watch competitive differentiation disappear.

Be ready for the difficult middle

Action -

- Define a transformational change process you will use when you get to Step Five of our programme.
- Understand how the difficult middle will impact your organisation.
- Be ready to be under water on the change curve.
- Work out how and when you will communicate.
- What are your benchmarks for success and progress?

I think the hardest part of growing into the CEO or business leader role is understanding how to hold the tension between leadership and management. Although they are very different, they are also intrinsically linked and it can be easy to end up caught between the two stools.

Alex Ferguson in his book *Leading* talks about how he gave up taking coaching sessions at Man Utd so he could observe more. He felt that he was better able to see how his players were feeling and looking by not getting quite so close. Martin O Neill in his time at Glasgow Celtic would often not be seen on the training ground all week, preferring to engage with the team at the pre-match briefings to give his words maximum impact. Theodore Roosevelt once said:

> *'The best leader is one who has sense enough to pick good people to do what he wants to be done, and self-restraint enough to keep from meddling with them while they do it.'*

All those are very valuable lessons in how not to become an obstacle to turning strategy into action.

So I have a question for you: are you talented enough to design yourself out of a job? I used to think that being a leader meant, well, leading. You're the boss; you run the company. A good CEO or leader is involved in all aspects of running the business, right? I have to stay on top of all the operations and all decision-making to be a good executive. That's how leaders roll. Except that I was wrong.

Eventually, I worked out the BEST leaders work in an inverted pyramid. Instead of all your employees working for you, you work for them. I understand now that the companies I ran were successful because we had the best team and often in spite of me. Getting the best team comes from building an environment where all the best people wanted to work. Instead of trying to 'run the company' and do everything myself, I started to spend my time hunting for talent. Bringing them on board, then constantly trying to see what I could do for them to make their job the best job they ever had, and make this company the best place they ever worked.

I learned to arrive at work not knowing quite what I was going to do that day. For sure the diary would have meetings in and for sure I would be focused on the performance of the organisation, but the biggest win you can have is the day you recognise you don't 'do stuff' anymore.

I started to plan my weeks around adding value without creating work; focusing on strategy, people, alignment, culture, communication, what's next for the organisation, and most importantly stakeholder management. It's hard but it's a liberating process to go through and one that was brought home to me at a recent job interview.

I was discussing a senior executive role with a big FTSE organisation, becoming CEO of an underperforming division. the Chairman who I was having dinner with suddenly came out with a statement, fully loaded... 'I hear you don't have a great work ethic.' BAM. Now for someone who considered himself to be the stereotypical alpha male, this was some statement, but I retained my composure. I sipped my wine, boiled inside, and sweetly slid a question back across the table.

I asked the Chairman, if I worked from six in the morning until ten at night seven days a week, took no holidays, and one year into the role things were worse, losses were bigger, stores looked less attractive, cash utilisation was higher, and staff were demoralised, would he fire me? Without blinking or pausing he said, 'I wouldn't wait a year to fire you.'

So I then said, if I worked five days a week starting around 8.30 and finishing by 6, visited stores on a Saturday, took all my holidays, didn't consider that I needed to be chained to the CEO's office all week and then one year into the role I had turned around the financial performance, built a new proposition for the business, created a culture of success, re-energised the team and returned the division to profit, would he pay me a huge bonus? His response was more measured this time, 'Yes, I could see that happening.'

'So why are we talking about my work ethic then? You are hiring me to add value not to do loads of work.'

Interestingly, I didn't get the job, but I made a point to him and the next day when I reflected on the meeting I realised I had also made a point to myself— a clear point about my leadership brand. I had transitioned to the place where I could focus on adding value not work.

Be prepared to do less and think more

Action -

- Are you clear about where you add the most value?
- Do you know how to get out of the way of the talented team you have put together?
- Are you focused enough on stakeholder management?
- Have you got enough time to think about what next?
- Are you constantly looking at strategy and opportunity?
- Are you focused on building the environment that will allow your team to flourish?

So that's Step Four finished. Let's recap on the key action points before we move on to *motivate*, *engage* and *mobilise* to create momentum.

Be clear about how you should lead the organisation

Action -

- Define your leadership brand and map out how this is relevant to your organisation.
- Work out how you can invest in your leadership style.
- What do you need to adapt?
- Find a solution by holding a mirror up to your face.
- Understand the impact your style has on others.
- Start using a profiling and communication tool with your Team One.
- Complete a 360 assessment and map behaviour changes from the results.

Be open to using different leadership styles at the right times

Action -

- Review your leadership style.
- How do you balance transformational with what got you here?
- How do you achieve the balance of old world/new world traits?
- What is your language to inspire your team with your vision?
- What are the no-compromise areas and does everybody understand them?
- What spots are going to get adapted?

Be ready for the difficult middle

Action -

- Define a transformational change process you will use when you get to Step Five of our programme.
- Understand how the difficult middle will impact your organisation.
- Be ready to be under water on the change curve.
- Work out how and when you will communicate.
- What are your benchmarks for success and progress?

Be prepared to do less and think more

Action -

- Are you clear about where you add the most value?
- Do you know how to get out of the way of the talented team you have put together?
- Are you focused enough on stakeholder management?
- Have you got enough time to think about what next?
- Are you constantly looking at strategy and opportunity?

Are you focused on building the environment that will allow your team to flourish?

It is easy to miss the importance of leadership in this journey to enhanced performance. We get our heads down and focus on delivering better results without truly appreciating how we can add value to our goal of making our business more successful. It's an easy mistake to make because the softer side of leadership is so intangible and as pace-setting business leaders we have achieved what we have achieved by being incredibly tangible with everything we do, measure, work hard, attain. It's the very core of what shapes our formative character, but in this new world, we need to recognise that this may not be how our talented people need us to behave.

**In Step Five: we will now identify some key actions you can
take to mobilise your organisation; to unleash the power of
the resource that is in the business, to create an unstoppable
force capable of delivering outstanding and lasting success,
to create the magic of *momentum*.**

When I finally realised in the mid-80s that I wasn't talented enough at
golf to be the next Seve, I moved to London and became the teaching
professional at South Herts GC in Totteridge.

In a way, making the change from playing to teaching was probably the
single decision that launched my business career. I just didn't know it
at the time. South Herts was a great club; one of London's oldest and
most respected golf clubs with a membership list of stars and celebs as
well as some excellent players. My teaching clientele included some
fantastic characters from showbiz and sport, Des O'Connor, Frankie
Vaughan, Barry Took, Jerry Stevens, Grace Kennedy from Arsenal
football club, Charlie Nicholas, Pat Jennings, Terry Neil, and their
manager George Graham...it was a fun time. I was in my mid-twenties
living in London and having a blast.

I taught for three seasons there and also built a strong network of both
local professionals, top class amateurs, and tour professionals who also
came to me for lessons and development on their games. This was
where I took my first formative steps in high potential performance
improvement and where I learned a very valuable lesson.

The club amateurs I taught, I soon realised, were all looking for the
silver bullet, the panacea, which could be trusted to cure all ills; the
magic secret, the one single piece of advice that would change their
game forever. Few realised that improving their game was a long,
drawn-out and sometimes painful process of change; with the high

possibility of getting worse before they got better and with the absolute fact that they would only get out proportionate to what they were prepared to put in. As Gary Player said, 'The more I practice, the luckier I get.'

The top players, on the other hand, realised that elevated performance levels came from a systematic approach to continuous improvement. They were prepared to work for hours on making the smallest detail right. Almost indistinguishable change to the naked eye would be perfected with hours on the range. They would dissect every round to see where the shots were given away and then together we would build a plan to improve, creating drills to enhance specific actions and swing changes.

But interestingly, although there were two very different approaches to performance improvement, when any player goes onto the golf course they need to be able to block out the technical stuff and have a single word or focus of concentration. This is quite a dichotomy; so much technical stuff swirling around in the head and yet the need to focus the mind on a single thought. I solved this for players by giving them a broad, sensing feeling to concentrate on. This lets the body do what it has just been trained to do; replicate an action. In golf, I would always get a player to focus on *rhythm* especially when the round or tournament was coming to an end and the pressure was on. It's not the silver bullet advice but it's the single most important factor when you take the game onto the course or tournament.

When I'd do presentations or work with businesses to improve performance levels, people would often ask what I believe to be the single most important factor in delivering the success that they were striving for. It is an interesting and challenging question and one that's quite easy to answer but in a qualified way.

Like with teaching golf, improving a business has no silver bullet. Nope, sorry, nada, niente, nicht, nothing. It's a continuous process of improvement that we have walked through in the first four steps of our programme. Small parts build into a powerful force, doing a hundred things 1% better, initiating and delivering change, creating culture, being focused on the right things. But, still, the human psyche wants the answer to their favourite question... What's that one thing?

So my answer is always the same…**Momentum.**

If you want to focus the business on achieving one single state that will make the difference, focus on delivering momentum throughout the organisation. For those of you who have read through the whole book, by now you will understand how to create momentum. Newton was quite specific, build the mass, direct force, remove opposites, increase the velocity…simple.

Step Five now focuses on how you *engage, motivate,* and *mobilise* your talented team to create a powerful unstoppable force that leads you to the success you are looking for.

Running a business is fun, isn't it? For sure there are always challenges and frustrations but on the whole, being a CEO or a business leader is a great job. It's fulfilling and rewarding to play a part in building a legacy that can be handed on down through the family, back to shareholders, or on to the team that you have spent years painstakingly putting together and developing. At some point, you will be able to settle into retirement and reflect on a life well spent. We are very lucky to do what we do.

I often reflect on the most challenging part of the CEO's year. Is it the annual budget review where you spend as little time as possible trying to sandbag next years' numbers as much as possible? Nah. Is it the company meeting where you have to stand up and once again tell staff the numbers don't look good? Nah. Is it the day you have to let someone go because it's just not working out having them as part of the team? Nah. All are challenging times, but these are events we have trained and developed our skillset to handle.

Without a doubt, in my experience, I always find the most challenging and stressful part of the CEO year is the shopping trip you make every December with your wife to find her dress for your company's Christmas dinner; that's real stress.

As business leaders, we are not conditioned to handle the level of emotion that always plays out during the trip. We would use our rational cognitive thinking to pick what we want. Need a party dress? What colour, what material, how long, what price, which brand, BOOF, in we go, pick the dress, and get back on with being successful.

What we experience is something entirely different. We go through the most incredible emotional journey of discovery, trying on numerous options in multiple stores across different styles, colours, fabrics, cuts, looks until we find THE ONE that delivers the emotional engagement that your wife is looking for. (Usually, the first one she tried on in the first shop!)

The lesson here is compelling, isn't it? Rather than start with what she is buying, if we can shift our mindset into **WHY** she is buying it then our capability to play a decisive part in the process is materially enhanced. At this point I am not going to put myself forward as a world leading expert on dress-buying psychology, but I think I understand enough to realise that the *why* part extends beyond 'I need a new dress' and is wrapped up in how I will feel when I wear it; will I feel sexy, sophisticated, and sultry?

In reality, when you are working towards heightened levels of employee engagement and motivation, don't the same factors all apply as the annual dress shopping trip? Emotional connections can determine the strength and length of a customer or an employee relationship. They drive passion, loyalty, and advocacy. Those same emotional connections will determine not just the strength and length of their time with you but also the level of commitment and value-added contribution.

In any organisation, all the people could tell you What we do, most of the people can tell you How we do it, but few know Why we do it...
-Simon Sinek

The product and marketing team at Karen Millen spend hours working at how to appeal to your wife's senses. Rational marketing is old school now. People don't buy rational features and benefits, they buy an emotional sensory experience. Using the limbic part of the brain to absorb the information needed they then merely check in with the prefrontal cortex to get a rational validation of their emotional decision to buy.

When employees decide whether to engage with your business, they use a similar process. Can they absorb the emotional and sensory messages and then get a rational validation? So much of what you need to do to drive enhanced performance is rational: plan, test, execute, appraise. But so much of what makes it happen successfully is down to engagement, motivation, and mobilisation of the team.

Sir Dave Brailsford

In this book, we have already looked at the renaissance in British cycling and also Team Sky and the TDF success, in both of which Sir Dave Brailsford played a significant part. Without wishing to make this a soliloquy to one individual, when I was researching examples of business leaders who had motivated organisations to deliver exceptional results and specifically to find examples of leaders who were able to articulate clearly to their employees the *why*, I came across this piece, written in 2015 by Brailsford. It is a review of the first five years of Team Sky and him setting out the vision for the next five.

I use it here because I think it is one of the finest examples of *why* I have ever seen and I found it impossible even to contemplate how anyone reading this could not fail to be inspired and motivated to deliver for both the leader and Team Sky. If this is an example of how he operates then, i) it Is not difficult to see why he has been so successful, and ii) I defy you after reading it to not want to work for him.

I have replicated it verbatim from the Team Sky website:

On the fifth anniversary of Team Sky, Team Principal Sir Dave Brailsford shares his vision for the next five years - **'2020 Vision'**

> It is five years since Team Sky was created. It is a good time to look back five years to the start of our journey in 2010 and an even better time to look forward to 2020 and the next big steps we hope to take. Today is not about giving all the detail. That will follow over the coming months. What it is about is setting the broad direction to achieve our '2020 vision'.

> When we first set out our objectives for Team Sky, they could not have been clearer. To win the greatest bike race in the world, within five years, to do it with a British rider, and do it clean. And in doing so to inspire a million more people to take up cycling.

> We met all of our objectives - ahead of schedule. We won the Tour de France twice. We won 165 races in total. We won them clean. We played a big part in the revolution of cycling as a great participation and spectator sport, especially in the UK, Team Sky's home, but elsewhere too.

The fact that we did manage to meet all of our objectives, on one level, is great. But in a culture like Team Sky's, which is built on constantly asking if we could do better, success means never resting on our laurels. I am immensely proud of the team but it is in our DNA always to think that we could have done more and pushed the boundaries further. And we learned a lot.

We learned that in a sport as competitive as this, you never stay ahead for long. So we must innovate better, smarter and faster. We have learned massive amounts about human performance, but there is still so much more we can do, and the opportunity for collaboration is vast. We also learned just how much people love cycling and how many more can fall in love with the bike. We learned about our role in education and drawing people into the passion of professional cycling.

Our 2020 mission is very simple - *for Team Sky to be indisputably and consistently the best cycling team in the world* - and to be viewed as one of the very best sports teams in the world.

But alongside that, and just as important, our vision is to play a leadership role in writing the next chapter for this great sport of ours: put the doping culture, and any tolerance of it, firmly into the past; write a future in which the world comes to see the best of cycling and acknowledges it for what it truly is:

> - the ultimate team sport
> - the ultimate stretch of human endurance and physical performance
> - the ultimate marriage of human and mechanical performance.

For me, professional cycling is still poorly appreciated - the athleticism and application of riders over sustained periods is unparalleled. And that is the tragedy of doping - it undermines a magnificent sport and belittles the achievements of the world's finest athletes. I want Team Sky to continue to help chart a brighter future for the sport.

So on the road to 2020: the three cornerstones of Team Sky remain exactly the same as they were five years ago:

Winning - we have to win the biggest races in the world consistently.

Performance - we have to innovate to push the boundaries of human performance and do it clean.

Inspiration - we have to make more people fall in love with cycling.

What is very different for this next chapter is the level of our aspiration and the ambitions for each element. The hunger is even greater to make sure that the next five years are even better than the last five years. We break this down into 'the what', 'the how' and 'the why':

Winning (The What)

If we are to be seen as the best cycling team over a decade, then we need to match those words with deeds that see medals round necks, and Team Sky riders on podiums wearing the famous jerseys of our sport. In 2020 when we look back over the decade we want Team Sky to be seen as the most consistent and successful Grand Tour team as well as one that is regularly winning Classics. It means more success over the next five years than the last five. In short, it means becoming the most complete global team, but a team with British roots that is continuously developing the best talent.

Performance (The How)

Certainly, we want to enter every race as the best prepared and most focused team. A team that has done everything conceivable to allow our riders to achieve their maximum potential. If we do that we will win races, including the greatest races in the world. We want Team Sky to be at the cutting edge of research and innovation - a reference point for excellence in human performance. We have gathered so much knowledge that we can use now and in the future, but that others can use too. We will have more to say about this in the course of the year. It means that over the coming years teams from other sports increasingly look to us for the methods and the thinking we use. A bit like now, we might look to F1 or the All Blacks or other great teams in sport.

It means too that we start to apply some of our thinking to other sports and even other industries, again as F1 has done for some years. And we want to continue to play a leadership role in charting a better future for this great sport and changing the culture that so damaged it. That means continued leadership on anti-doping.

Inspiration (The Why)

Our ultimate purpose is very simple - to do everything that we can to make more people fall in love with the sport so it can have a positive impact on their lives. Participation in cycling and interest in the sport has grown enormously at every level over recent years. Millions more are riding bikes. The massive crowds at Le Grand Depart in Yorkshire showed the level of interest in the sport and made it one of the best days of my life.

Cycling is an amazing sport as it allows everyone to experience the thrill of riding - from the child on their first bike to the keen amateur. It can be a force for good in so many ways from health to the environment and the economy. Cycling is growing fast. The opportunities are huge. We need to continue to lead the way and help make cycling the number one sport of choice for millions globally. It means opening up the sport so people can appreciate it for what it is - the ultimate team sport and test of athleticism and endurance.

We are a data rich sport. In F1, data is part of the story. It has become part of the spectacle. It can be the same in our sport. Of course all teams have information about their riders, their strategies, their tactics, that they want to keep under wraps. Where you have or can develop a competitive advantage, you want to keep it. But that should not blind us to the mass of information we could make public, including in real time, in a way that would add to the media and spectator appreciation of the sport.

There is something spell binding about seeing a rider break away from the pack on a climb. But what if we could actually know what exactly was happening to the bike, and to the body pedalling it, at that time? How much richer would the experience of following the sport be? Again, we will have more to say on this. The initiative with Velon is only the start - we applaud the collaboration between the professional teams to strengthen our sport through a shared vision to get more fans closer to cycling.

By 2020 I want Team Sky to be recognised as a beacon of sporting excellence after a decade of sustained success. And how we have done it matters just as much as what we have done. But above all, why we have done it matters most of all - for the love of cycling.

Sir Dave Brailsford

11/01/2015

For me, this is a benchmark in emotional and engaging communication with all your stakeholders. Ask yourselves now, fresh from reading the passage, do you have something equally as compelling and motivational that you have shared with your employees?

Do we start with *why*?

Action -

- Does the understanding *of* why extend far enough through the organisation?
- Is the senior team focused on tapping into emotional engagement rather than just rational action?
- Have you thought through the language and sensory prompts you can use to influence others?
- Is VPA clearly definable?
- Do people understand what a high-performance culture looks like?
- Is your *why* inspirational?

I don't know if you have ever been and holidayed in Scotland. If you have, the chances are you will have taken the opportunity to head up past Loch Lomond, drive through Glencoe, the mighty U-shaped Glen formed by ice age glaciers and infamous for the Glencoe massacre of 1692 and visit the wonderful area of the Highlands that is Fort William, home to the highest peak in Britain, Ben Nevis.

It's a breathtakingly beautiful journey once you get north of Glasgow. Following the bonny, bonny banks of Loch Lomond and as you drive further north, opening out into some of the most inspiring views you will see anywhere in the world; culminating in your first sight of the *Three Sisters*, the shoulders of the Bidean nam Bian massif, which guard the western end of the glen and signal your arrival into a walker's paradise. Truly Awesome.

In 1994, I had just joined a small camping company called Vango, it was my first real job at senior executive level; great brand, magical heritage, privately owned by the Moodie family and was what I would call a 'traditional West of Scotland business' no airs, no graces, just made great products to do what the customer wanted them to do. I started as sales director and within six months became the new MD upon the retirement of Alistair Moodie Sr., an uncle of the family owners.

The business was small, around £5m turnover, if I remember correctly. It was a bit stuck in its ways, profitability was OK but, remember, this was Scotland, and every penny has a real value up there! It probably hadn't moved forward in its offer and proposition over the previous few years, but the sentiment of both its retail customers and the consumer was still very positive.

My brief was to grow and expand the business. This is where I first started to form the Fresh Oxygen Five-Step Programme. I just had no idea at the time that I was doing it. Working on instinct and intuition, I started to build a new business plan. With the board, we looked at current performance and worked out where and how we saw the scope to enhance it.

We developed a new strategic plan, made some choices and produced what we thought back then were some pretty glitzy PowerPoint slides to promote it. We explored the team and worked out what competencies and capabilities we were short of and set out to bring the right people in. We talked long into the night about culture and performance and how to improve it, and I probably, although I was not conscious of doing it, thought a little bit about my leadership style and how this traditional Scottish business would respond to a 'Sassenach' being in charge.

At this point, we wanted to share our new plan with the broader team. I probably didn't use the language *engage, motivate and mobilise to create momentum* back then. I probably said, 'Let's share this with the team,' but the principle was there.

Hence we all found ourselves in the shadow of Ben Nevis. Where better to take a great British climbing company to share the board's new plan? We took everyone up, stayed in a great Scottish holiday-style hotel; you know the ones, fantastic choice of whisky, incredible breakfast of everything and always haggis included, little bit tired to look at but full of charisma and presented the new world as we saw it...Brilliant Plan.

At lunchtime after the morning session, I was congratulating myself on how well it had gone. The plan felt coherent; the presentation was clear; I was in good form, inspirational and motivational; everybody got it; nothing could stop us now. Then one of my sales guys approached me and hit me with another BAM moment.

'When are you going to show them what's in it for them?' he asked me. BAM! again. A simple question but one that in all the time we had worked through the plan we hadn't spent much time on. It was a simple lesson that I have never forgotten and probably was the single line to shape Step Five of our programme. It was this experience that forms the base of being engaging and motivating. People work for businesses and jobs for many different reasons. For sure, money is one, but we all know it is not the primary motive.

As generational terminology has developed over the last thirty years, we have become inundated with advice and insight into the motivators of our workforce. **Baby Boomers** are accepted to be economically optimistic, idealistic, individualistic, prefer achievement over relations, competitive, and with a willingness to say in the same company for a long period of time (being a baby boomer myself I can relate to that). The new Millennials or **Generation Y** are technology-reliant, image-driven, multitasking, open to change, team-oriented, information rich, impatient, adaptable, and seek personal growth, meaningful careers, and mentors or supervisors to encourage and facilitate their professional development.

Sandwiched in-between is **Generation X**, born in the 70s and early 80s. They make up 60% of the workforce and typically will possess more of an entrepreneurial spirit, a do-it-yourself attitude and, in contrast to the generations before them, they are way more likely to embrace change in the workplace. They are career-oriented but place a healthy emphasis on family time and strive for a good work-life balance. They possess a different work ethic to the boomers; Gen X thrives on diversity, challenge, responsibility, honesty, and creative input, compared to the boomers' preference for a more rigid, work-centric approach.

My point here is not to educate you on generation terminology; there is a whole internet out there that could occupy you for days. My point here is, before you start the process of communicating the new world plan, ask yourself this, 'Given the profile of my workforce, how can I change the culture and environment to deliver more what's-in-it-for-me motivators?'

You will have a diverse employee base spread across all three generations. If you are a traditional business you are likely to be more reliant on baby boomers, creative and services tend to be populated by Gen X and new technology will be heavily dependent on the New Millennials. Each wants something different but, for sure, we know that each wants something.

While many people talk about profits and productivity as the necessary ingredients:
I believe that a business' long-term success is built on staff who love working there and customers who love the company's products or services

-Richard Branson

We also know that only 30% of our workforce is engaged in what we are trying to achieve. Our job as business leaders is to find the levers and the tools that turn this number on its head, and it can be done. It takes time and thought and a sustained approach to being real and authentic, to delivering the environment you say you will provide, and to creating the culture you say you will create; to making engagement and motivation at the very forefront of your higher purpose and not something that you scratch your head about once a year when you read the latest employee survey results.

As a footnote, when I left the business in 2001, turnover had reached £20m+ and we had won numerous business awards in the West of Scotland, Growth Business of the Year two times, Marketing Business of the year once, I had won Businessman of the Year once and been a finalist a second time. I am insanely proud that this company went on to top £100m and did so with pretty much the same board and broadly the same team as was in place from the very beginning. The sales guy who asked me the 'what's in it for them?' question is now the CEO and in 2013 orchestrated an MBO from the shareholders.

How *engaged* is our workforce

Action -

- Map the generation profile of your employees.
- Build a *what's-in-it-for-me* matrix.
- Understand the drivers of the emotional connection and culture you are looking for.
- Map your engaged-employee-ratio and set targets for the future.
- Make VPA come alive in the organisation.

- Create clear development plans for people.
- Work on delivering flexibility, autonomy, and a sense of ownership.

The first time I went to Pentland head office (HO) in Finchley to meet Andy Rubin, I was blown away by the place. It was the most incredible work environment I had ever seen. Not just the physical infrastructure, which in itself was impressive, but the whole approach to creating a workspace that would appeal to the motivators of its employees.

The family had over-invested in the environment to ensure that they were fully optimised with talent. The business owns and licenses some fantastic brands—JD Sports, Lacoste, Speedo, Berghaus, Ted Baker footwear, Canterbury, Mitre, Ellesse, Heidi Klein, Hunter, Kickers, Boxfresh and others. The list is endless and the HO is packed with Gen X and Gen Y people all incredibly motivated and engaged with both the group and their brands.

One of the core values of the family and the business is *'to be a great place to work'* and they certainly walk the talk. In 2014, the Great Place to Work Institute named Pentland as one of the Top 10 best places to work in the UK and Top 20 in Europe. In 2003, when the new corporate headquarters was completed, it was voted the best corporate workplace in the UK. In 2008, Pentland was voted the best family business in the UK by the Institute for Family Business and in 2014, won Top European Family Business of the Year at the European Families in Business Awards.

The business has 19,000 employees worldwide in over 100 countries and in last year's Global Employee Survey over 80% of respondents said Pentland is a great place to work. Pentland received two accolades at CIPD People Management Awards in 2014 for Overall Winners and Best Employee Engagement Initiative. These awards recognise an innovative and engaging approach to the development of their people and commend the people-centred culture across their business.

Am I making a point?

Creating the right atmosphere is a huge part of delivering momentum, but it's a continuous process. It is not about putting a few buzzword posters up around the place (although Pentland has plenty of these). It is a systematic approach to delivering an environment where people are inspired to be the best they can be, and this has to be driven by the CEO or business leader. Andy Rubin can articulate it way better than me;

> **'We are family** - When you join Pentland, you're joining an exciting global business that's built on strong family values.
>
> There are perhaps many companies that claim to be led by family values, but we're the real deal. As a family-owned business, for three generations we have applied family values, supporting our people while giving them the freedom to innovate and become the best they can be in their work.
>
> **United in our values** - Ours is a global and diverse family. We have more than 19,000 employees worldwide. In the UK alone, we have people of seventeen different nationalities, speaking twenty-three languages. Our global teams are united in a mutual respect and a desire to move the business forever forward.
>
> **Investing in our joint future** - When you work for us, we invest in your professional development - after all, the whole company shares in your successes. In return, we ask that you complement your skills and knowledge with the ambition to achieve, the courage to suggest new ideas, and the desire to seek improvements in everything we do.'

Powerful stuff and for sure the physical infrastructure plays a part; nice swimming pool to test the Speedos, cool shop to buy all the brands in, chill out area to play pool or table tennis, a great gym, brilliant canteen, five-a-side pitch for Mitre to play in their new products. I can go on but I guess I don't really need to, the point is that if you went into Pentland right now and conducted a simple employee engagement survey, one question: Are you engaged, not engaged or disengaged? Do you think the ratio would be 30/50/20 like the national average? Nah, not a chance!

In 2016, total revenue increased to £2.4 billion, up 10%; group profit was up 36% to £220m, and net cash increased by over £100m. All this is a testimony to getting the environment right.

Without a shadow of a doubt, Pentland is the best organisation I have ever worked for. A combination of environment, approach to its people and giving you the space to maximise your talent results in high levels of engagement but also a workplace where company success actually means something tangible to you.

Zappos - the rise and rise of a customer service company which happens to sell shoes

When Tony Hsieh (pronounced Shay) graduated from college, he got a job at Oracle. But after a few months he found that he didn't care much for the corporate culture, so he left the company to start his own business, LinkExchange. For the first few years, Hsieh enjoyed working at his new business because he would hire his friends or friends of friends, and everyone got along. But the company soon ran into a problem: they needed more people, and they had run out of friends to hire.

He tried hiring other people, but somehow it just didn't work. They might be competent and with the right skillset but invariably they didn't seem to fit the LinkExchange culture. By the time the company grew to 100 employees, the culture had been lost and Hsieh, who by this time was struggling to find the motivation to go to work, was happy to accept a big cheque from Microsoft in 1998 to acquire his business.

He invested some of the cash into an online shoe retailer called Shoesite.com. His idea was to be a passive investor but quickly he realised he missed the day-to-day involvement. He started to work as the CEO, changed the name to Zappos (a variation of the Spanish word zapatos meaning shoes) and vowed that the new business, unlike LinkExchange would never lose its sense of company culture.

Hsieh wanted Zappos to become the pinnacle of online customer service.

The original business model was to take the styles of shoe that their branded partners had in their warehouses and offer them on the Zappos website. Once an order was taken the brand would ship directly to the customer. Hsieh soon realised that this was a flawed model and would not allow Zappos to offer outstanding customer service, so they made some key decisions.

They would only sell stock they had in their warehouse, they would give the call centre customer service reps the power to make any decision, and they would get the warehouse to operate 24/7, 365 days a year. This might be inefficient, yes, but it was the key to fast delivery to customers, making the customer the centre of the business model, and it has worked.

After minimal gross sales in 1999, Zappos brought in $1.6 million in revenue in 2000. In 2001, sales more than quadrupled to $8.6 million. Three years later in the financial year 2004, the business recorded $184 million in gross sales and received their first round of venture capital funding, a $35 million investment from Sequoia Capital. That same year, they moved their headquarters from San Francisco to Las Vegas and over the next three years, Zappos continued to double their annual revenues, hitting $840 million in gross sales by 2007 and expanding the product offer to include handbags, eyewear, clothing, watches, and kids' merchandise.

> **'Zappos is a customer service company**
> **that just happens to sell shoes.'**
> *-Tony Hsieh*

In 2008, Zappos hit $1 billion in annual sales, two years earlier than expected. On 22 July 2009, Amazon announced that it would buy Zappos for $940 million in a stock and cash deal. The deal was eventually closed in November 2009 for a reported $1.2 billion.

The deal made the shareholders and also the employees extremely wealthy people, but the impressive point is that in building a $1 billion organisation from nothing in ten years, Hsieh never lost sight of keeping the company culture consistent and true to its values.

'Our number one priority is company culture. Our whole belief is that if you get the culture right, most of the other stuff like delivering great customer service or building a long-term enduring brand will just happen

naturally on its own.'
-Tony Hsieh

There are dozens of stories about their outstanding customer service, including delivering flowers to a customer whose mum had passed away and talking to a customer for eight hours about which products to buy. It should come as no surprise given the zeal with which customer service is at the forefront of the business model that 75% of Zappos orders are from repeat customers.

But to achieve this level of customer service you have to have a culture that is quite extraordinary and this is where Hsieh demonstrates he is extraordinary. In his fascinating autobiography *Delivering Happiness* Hsieh clearly articulates how he built this incredibly consistent and durable culture.

In the early days of Zappos, Hsieh interviewed every job applicant. This was his way of protecting the culture and ensuring the right people were hired, but this was clearly unsustainable as the business grew. To ensure that the culture was maintained, Hsieh built a two-stage recruitment process.

Firstly, a competency assessment; does the candidate have the skill set and capability to handle the role interviews? The second part focused on would they be someone that Hsieh would like to know personally? Hsieh would ask himself: *'Is this someone I would choose to hang out with or grab a drink with...if we weren't in business together? If the answer is no, then we wouldn't hire them.'* Sometimes these interviews would involve vodka shots to loosen people up and see how strong the emotional connection was.

Jim Collins in his book *From Good to Great* says that one of the key differentiators separating great companies from good companies is how strong and distinctive the company culture is.

Hsieh embraced this at Zappos, establishing a clear set of core values that were then used to define the company culture. Interestingly, over time, he came to the conclusion that it mattered less what the values were but more that Zappos had them and were aligned behind them. Hsieh believed the power came from the alignment, not from the actual words.

The recruitment process became the most important piece of maintaining and sustaining the Zappos culture. Hire people that fit and are engaged with the values, don't hire competency and then try to mould to the culture.

Even now at $1b+ revenue, Zappos' method of hiring hasn't changed much since Hsieh was personally interviewing candidates. They do two sets of interviews with each candidate. The hiring manager and their team do a round of competency interviews to make sure the person is skilled, and then HR does their interviewing to ensure the person is a culture fit. The applicant must pass both interview rounds, or they are not offered a role.

Every new Zappos employee goes through the same four-week training process. They learn the company strategy, the culture, why it's important to the future of the business, and they are indoctrinated in the customer service philosophy. Everyone spends two weeks in the call centre, building an appreciation of the Zappos customer and their requirements.

At some point during the training, Zappos offers $4,000 to the new employee to quit and walk away from the company. Think about this, they are only a few weeks into a new business; the HR team has spent time and money driving the recruitment process, his people have invested their expertise in making the decision, and Hsieh offers the new recruit $4k to go away. Unbelievable!

Hsieh says they don't want people who are there for a paycheck, and they don't want people who feel like they are trapped. He says that the percentage of people who take the money is 2-3%. When new employees turn down the money, they prove to be much more passionate and engaged because they realise that it's a place they want to be and contribute in.

To this day, they continue to turn down talented individuals who don't fit the culture, no matter how smart, no matter how big the potential contribution to the organisation might be. Similarly, if someone slips through the recruitment net but proves through time not to get the business and its values, they fire the individual no matter how good they are. Performance reviews are 50% based on living the Zappos culture.

And the culture is unique!

In reception, there is a throne and visitors get to sit in it and feel that at Zappos the customer is truly king. Every person gets to decorate their desk or department work areas with themes and props everywhere. When visitors tour the building the staff greet them by ringing cowbells. It's a zany, crazy, amazing environment but one that people love working in.

It almost has a feel of a religious sect to it, and it's definitely not right for everyone. Zappos is an outstanding example of using culture and values to inspire an organisation to deliver exceptional service and results. If you get the chance, visit the Zappos website and experience some of the company videos for yourself; it is inspirational stuff.

Contrast this approach to the Jack Welch Rank and Yank approach that we looked at in Step Three: Building a high-performance culture. If ever you needed a tangible demonstration of there being more than one way to reach your summit then these are the two extreme examples and yet both in their way have delivered rapid performance improvement and sustainable success.

How much conclusive data there is between enhanced engagement levels and improved financial results is debatable. There are lots of studies and research papers to be read, and most will indicate a big and getting bigger percentage progress. As Benjamin Disraeli once said, 'There are lies, damn lies and statistics,' and for me, this is one of those areas.

Don't try to pin a figure on measuring the tangible benefit of enhanced employee engagement; it is like trying to pick your wife's dress for the Christmas party. This is a trust moment, not a measure moment. If you believe that you have recruited an amazing team and if you believe they have the desire and the commitment to make it happen, then create the environment they need and let them get on with it...I promise you the results will follow.

Is our business a *great* place to work?

Action -

- Is the company culture and are the company values the driver of environment?
- Review five key areas of the environment you are creating for your team;
  - o Is their work meaningful? Is the job fit right [0]and do they have the tools and autonomy to succeed?
  - o Do you have great management? Are goals and objectives clear? Do people feel supported? Is there clear development in place?
  - o Is it a positive work environment: does it feel inclusive, flexible and physically inspiring?
  - o Are there opportunities for growth: do you stretch the best? Are promotion and progress visible?
  - o Do the leaders demonstrate vision, purpose and transparency? Do you feel authentic, is it consistent and do the team feel they matter to you

Being a Global CEO is actually quite a neat job, maybe not quite right up there with being an astronaut, a Hollywood movie star, the presenter of Match of the Day, or even being the guy who taste tests Guinness at the brewery in Dublin. But all things considered, it's a pretty good way to earn a living.

You have a reasonable amount of autonomy to plan your working schedule, which will always involve significant periods of overseas travel. This, of course, has its perks. You always get to turn left when boarding intercontinental flights and you visit some amazing countries and engage with super interesting local people. You usually get to stay in five-star business hotels -clearly for efficiency purposes—, you experience other cultures and can absorb their influences and drivers. You get to broaden your knowledge and understanding of what and how different people tick.

I found it fascinating.

Which brings me to Moscow, January 2012. I had always wanted to visit Russia having grown up through the period of the dissolution of the USSR, the introduction of Glasnost and Perestroika and the end of the Cold War, but it had never quite made it to the top of my holiday list. As we were looking at potential partner options for Berghaus for Russia I had the chance to visit, review options and business plans. As I always did before leaving for a new country, I spent a little time researching culture, history, and people so that I was at least a little briefed before getting there.

This brings me to Mikhail Gorbachev, one of the great transformational leaders of the modern world.

Gorbachev was born in the small village of Privolnoye in the Stavropol territory. Both his grandparents and his parents were peasant farmers and after Stalin's collectivization programme, his father became a combine harvester driver. In a brave move, Gorbachev studied law at

Moscow State University. He joined the Communist Party and embarked on a career in politics. On 11 March 1985, Gorbachev became the General Secretary of the Central Committee of the Communist Party of the Soviet Union. At 54, he was now the leader of the Soviet Union.

Now, I don't think it appropriate to try to claim credit here for the transformational reforms that Gorbachev implemented but let's walk through what he did. My guess is he had already identified the position the USSR was in before he took the role and given the speed that he implemented change he had already made his strategic choices before taking office. He clearly assembled a high-performance team around him and built a culture of change and looking back now, it is easy to see how he shaped his leadership brand both within the USSR and also for the world stage.

If you stop for a brief minute and think what he then did and the speed at which he did it, we get one of the great lessons of the book.

He shocked many Soviet citizens when he announced the ability for citizens to freely voice their opinions, Glasnost, and the need to entirely restructure the Soviet Union's economy, Perestroika. Gorbachev also opened the door to allow Soviet citizens to travel, cracked down on alcohol abuse, and pushed for the use of computers and technology and released many political prisoners.

'The biggest single problem with Communication, is the illusion that it has taken place'
-George Bernard Shaw

For decades, the United States and the Soviet Union had been competing with each other over who could amass the largest, most lethal cache of nuclear weapons. As the United States was developing the new Star Wars program, Gorbachev realised that the Soviet Union's economy was seriously suffering from the excessive spending on nuclear weapons. To end the arms race, Gorbachev met several times with then US President Ronald Reagan.

Making progress at these meetings was a challenging and slow process. Trust between the two countries was limited and although both

Gorbachev and Reagan were able to identify the benefits of working out a solution, neither could appear to have backed down in the eyes of the world. Eventually, the two men reached a deal that would see not just an end to the manufacture of nuclear weapons but also a process of scrapping many that were already in service. The beginning of the end of the Cold War had started.

Although Gorbachev's economic, social, and political reforms as well as his warm, honest, friendly, open demeanour, won him accolades from around the world, including the Nobel Peace Prize in 1990, he was criticised by many within the Soviet Union. For some, his reforms had been too big and too fast; for others, his reforms had been too small and too slow. In 1991, he resigned, the day before the USSR state was dissolved.

Through all the change and through all the turmoil that he led the USSR, the one consistent thing he displayed was an amazing ability to communicate his vision, to communicate effectively and consistently, to shape sentiment and then to communicate again to reinforce the message and progress. He had a style that was open, honest, sometimes direct but always believable. He was able to carry the positive sentiment of the people of Russia with him, which was vital to achieving his goals and objectives.

And interestingly, he was able to shape this communication successfully, both style and message, for the rest of the world too and not just his own country.

We call this Communicate3, communicate the key vision, communicate again to shape the sentiment of all stakeholders, communicate again to reinforce the message and demonstrate progress. If you have successfully followed the framework of our Five Step Programme, then this is the final and most important step.

We have identified in the book how essential effective communication is as a component of a leader's success. Across your organisation, whether it is at the interpersonal, intergroup, intragroup, organisational, or external level, being able to succinctly communicate your message with maximum impact is a defining attribute for success. While developing an understanding of excellent communication skills is easier than you might think, being able to appropriately draw upon these skills when the chips are down is not always as easy as you might hope for. It is precisely this paradox that underscores the need for leaders to focus on becoming great communicators.

The number one thing great communicators have in common is they possess a heightened sense of situational and contextual awareness. They can fully concentrate on listening, absorbing what others are saying and not just preparing their response.

Remember my lesson from Ashridge!

Great communicators are skilled at reading an audience, by sensing the moods, dynamics, attitudes, values and concerns of others. A strong communicator will identify nonverbal clues and interactions and make the session a two-way process. Not only do they read their environment well, but they possess the uncanny ability to adapt their messaging to said environment without missing a beat; to connect and engage with the audience, to relate on a receivable wavelength and not dictate on an unbelievable waveband.

Understanding that the communication objective is not about the messenger is everything. This process has nothing to do with you, the messenger; it is, however, 100% about meeting the needs and the expectations of those you're communicating with.

Communication skills are another area where you need to invest your time and money to develop your skill set and capability. Once you have transitioned from creating work to adding value, your approach to Communicate3 will be the single biggest influence on building momentum across your organisation. All leaders need to shape and define their communication style; there is no cookie cutter solution, no template to follow, no single silver bullet!

My own style has evolved into a three-stage process, hence Communicate3.

I believe that Stage One is about education. It needs to be genuine and correct, rooted in clear business logic; the message should be simple but grounded in customer and market insight; the core message must have clarity and be easy to take away; it needs to articulate the vision, purpose, and ambition clearly.

I believe Stage Two is about inspiring. It needs to touch and win the hearts and minds; it must be engaging and delivered with empathy, not ego. You need to be a real person telling a compelling story; it needs to be believable, exciting, and to some extent out of reach but still tangible. It must have a strong sense of *why* and be deep in meaning.

I believe Stage Three is about reinforcement. It needs to be consistent and repeated; no big launch and disappear event. You need to be visible, positively repetitive, and tangible. This is not about you, your opinions, your circumstances, or your position. This is now about helping others by meeting their needs, understanding their concerns, and adding value to their world. It must demonstrate progress and recognise challenge while building confidence in delivery.

So, how do you know when your skills have matured to the point that you've become an excellent communicator? It's hard to answer this question but when your organisation and its people believe in you and your message as much as you believe in you and your message...then start to feel you might just be getting closer!

'People will forget what you said and did, but they will never forget how you made them feel.'
-Maya Angelou

Your role now in the process is to motivate and mobilise your team, turn them into truly your biggest asset, and shift the engagement ratio across your business. *What*, *how*, and *when* you communicate becomes the single biggest driver of delivering enhanced performance. Never underestimate the power you have at this stage; the power to inspire and excite.

Do we deliver our messages with *impact*?

Action -

- Map out the content, frequency and style of your communication plan.
- Define the key messages and repeat for consistency.
- Make sure there is a healthy dose of '*what's in it for me*' included.

- Think through delivery, the tough messages, and how you will communicate through the difficult middle stage.
- Develop your communication and presentation style for impact.

Let's recap Step Five and the key action points before we finalise the programme with some clear conclusions.

Do we start with *why*?

Action -

- Does the understanding *of* why extend far enough through the organisation?
- Is the senior team focused on tapping into emotional engagement rather than just rational action?
- Have you thought through the language and sensory prompts you can use to influence others?
- Is VPA clearly definable?
- Do people understand what a high-performance culture looks like?
- Is your *why* inspirational?

How *engaged* is our workforce

Action -

- Map the generation profile of your employees.
- Build a *what's-in-it-for-me* matrix.
- Understand the drivers of the emotional connection and culture you are looking for.
- Map your engaged-employee-ratio and set targets for the future.
- Make VPA come alive in the organisation.
- Create clear development plans for people.
- Work on delivering flexibility, autonomy, and a sense of ownership.

Is our business a *great* place to work?

Action -

- Is the company culture and are the company values the driver of environment?
- Review five key areas of the environment you are creating for your team;
  - o Is their work meaningful? Is the job fit right [0]and do they have the tools and autonomy to succeed?
  - o Do you have great management? Are goals and objectives clear? Do people feel supported? Is there clear development in place?
  - o Is it a positive work environment: does it feel inclusive, flexible and physically inspiring?
  - o Are there opportunities for growth: do you stretch the best? Are promotion and progress visible?
  - o Do the leaders demonstrate vision, purpose and transparency? Do you feel authentic, is it consistent and do the team feel they matter to you

Do we deliver our messages with *impact*?

Action -

- Map out the content, frequency and style of your communication plan.
- Define the key messages and repeat for consistency.
- Make sure there is a healthy dose of *'what's in it for me'* included.
- Think through delivery, the tough messages, and how you will communicate through the difficult middle stage.
- Develop your communication and presentation style for impact.

'Never underestimate the power of a small group of people to change the world, in fact, it is the only thing which ever has.'

The above is a quote by Margaret Mead, an American cultural anthropologist, and has become a bit of a mantra for me over the years. I think that it perfectly encapsulates the power of momentum, the capability to make change happen, and deliver progress for the future. When you are able to create the correct environment for your teams and engage, motivate, and mobilise them, then you will have achieved the single most important part of our programme: you will have created an unstoppable force and one that will be able to lead you to the success that you are set out to achieve.

At the heart of this book is the following message, that as successful CEOs or business leaders we have a difficult, complex, but, none the less, exciting role in preparing the companies we direct to progress in the future. The world is a constantly evolving place, with an infinite number of subtly changing dynamics on a daily basis and the challenge to us is to be able to identify and take advantage of the ones that provide us with opportunity.

The hardest part for me was learning the lesson to step outside of doing and spend the majority of my time on thinking; to spend less time on now and more time on the future; to shift my mindset from making it happen; to transform the organisation; to stop thinking of myself as the decision-making *boss* and start behaving as a facilitator.

In essence, the lesson was for me to become an agent of change and a transformational leader.

I am not suggesting here that you throw out all the good things and the strong personality traits that have made you and your business the success that you both undoubtedly are. Build on them with other strong attributes, keep the focus on performance and delivery, and learn how to complement them with leadership and engagement.

'The successful person begins with two fundamental beliefs: the future can be better than the present, and I have the power to make it happen.'

To close, I contend again that running a business successfully is not that difficult, that being a leader is the best job in the world, and that having a framework to build through the five steps will lead you to challenge the norm and banish the mediocrity.

As leaders we have a responsibility to deliver or provide an environment that allows the people who work for our organisation or company the best chance to be successful; to deliver a culture within which they can express their capability; and a direction and a vision that they find both compelling and inspiring. We have a responsibility to instil a sense of pride and ownership in what they do and what the business is trying to be, real clarity on what the organisation needs from them as individuals, and a clear sense of what good looks like.

My final thought to leave you with is the quote that has shaped so much of what I do:

In the climbing world there is a saying, *'the summit never comes to you'*, from where I know not, but it beautifully encapsulates the core of my learning about life, about being successful in whatever you set out to do, and the core of this book. As individuals, we are blessed with amazing power, capacity, and endurance. We have an infinite reservoir from which to draw on in order to achieve, and the only constraints are the ones we impose on ourselves.

Hold tightly the desire, the belief and the commitment that you can go reach your summit— whatever you define it to be. It may not come to you but, for sure, there is nothing in the world that can stop you getting to it.

So we reach the end of the Fresh Oxygen five step programme to enhanced performance improvement, increased value creation, and the success you aspire to. I hope that you have enjoyed reading our book, that it has prompted you to think about the art of the possible, that it has challenged your intellect and your reasoning, and that it has given you some ideas, tools, and techniques to transform your organisation.

I wish you every success on your journey and would love to hear back from you with your stories and experiences of what has worked for you. If I, or any of the team at Fresh Oxygen, can help you in your pursuit of being the best you can be, then do not hesitate to contact us. You can get me at richard@freshoxygen.co.uk or email zebra@freshoxygen.co.uk and you can visit our website at www.freshoxygen.co.uk . We will get right back to you.

Born in the Midlands in 1961, Richard Cotter excelled at sport at school, playing six different sports at representative level and honing a fiercely competitive nature. His academic career was somewhat less successful and he left High School at seventeen with few qualifications, following his dream to play professional sport.

For a period of eight years, he built a career as a professional golfer, playing European Tour events but really excelling as a teacher of club, celebrity, tour professional, and high calibre amateur golfers.

His first move into corporate life came when he joined the House of Fraser Department Store Group in 1986, progressing rapidly to a group buyer role and within a couple of years taking up the position of managing director of a subsidiary company of Beales Department Store Group at the tender age of twenty-eight. Subsequent positions followed: managing director of Vango at thirty-two, divisional managing director of AMG at thirty-five, managing director of Falcon Foodservice Group, followed by a ten-year period as the brand president and global CEO of Berghaus, building the eponymous British outdoor brand from the UK's leading name to a retail $300m true global player.

In 2013, he joined the Snow&Rock Group as CEO. Recruited by LGV Capital, the private equity arm of Legal & General to position the £100m turnover business for disposal, he successfully sold the company to PAI Partners in May 2015, securing the future of the business and the jobs of over 1000 employees.

He is now chairman and CEO of the Fresh Oxygen strategic consultancy, chairman of the ITM Group, chairman of Grace Cole Ltd, chairman of the Jack Wolfskin Group, a highly accomplished motivational speaker and a high-performance individual mentor.

Sport still plays a major part in his life but during his time with Berghaus and through a strong friendship with Sir Chris Bonington, the chairman of the Berghaus brand, Richard discovered climbing and high altitude mountaineering, both of which have become a passion. In 2005, he summited Kilimanjaro in Tanzania, at 5895m the highest freestanding point on the planet. Subsequent years have seen him summit via the Aiguille du Midi route, Mont Blanc at 4809m the highest peak in Europe and numerous other alpine peaks and rock walls, Cotopaxi at 5897m in Ecuador, and climbed to over 7000m in the Himalaya on Mera Peak and Baruntse.

He has a unique ability to correlate the risk and adventure of high altitude mountaineering, professional sport, and elite performance coaching with the risk and adventure of running businesses in corporate life. Drawing parallels that deliver success in both fields and articulating them in a pragmatic and actionable way.

In November 2014, he was diagnosed with lung cancer and faced life-threatening surgery. Subsequent diagnoses have resulted in treatment for cancer of the spine and multiple brain tumours. He has battled cancer with the same resilience and pragmatism that he has used to successfully achieve so many goals and objectives in his sporting, climbing, and business life.

He lives in Surrey with his partner, Irene, and son, Aidan.

Acknowledgements

Articles

The First Job of a Leader is to Face Reality - George Ambler. (n.d.). Retrieved from www.georgeambler.com/the-first-job-of-a-leader-is-to-face-reality/

How GB Cycling Went from Tragic to Magic - BBC News. (n.d.). Retrieved from http://news.bbc.co.uk/sport2/hi/olympics/cycling/7534073.stm

Peter Keen: Interview | Cyclist. (n.d.). Retrieved from www.cyclist.co.uk/news/142/peter-keen-interview

Momentum - Physics Classroom. (n.d.). Retrieved from www.physicsclassroom.com/Class/momentum/u4l1a.cfm

About Harley-Davidson | Harley-Davidson USA. (n.d.). Retrieved from www.harley-davidson.com/content/h-d/en_US/company.html

History | Warby Parker. (n.d.). Retrieved from www.warbyparker.com/history

The IKEA Vision - IKEA. (n.d.). Retrieved from www.ikea.com/ms/en_CA/the_ikea_story/working_at_ikea/our_vision.html

Case Study Analysis | Myles' Blog. (n.d.). Retrieved from https://mamelendez.wordpress.com/case-study-analysis/

case-analysis.wikispaces.com. (n.d.). Retrieved from https://case-analysis.wikispaces.com/file/view/Harley-Davidson+Final+Copy.doc

The first ascent of the Southwest Face of Everest? Mark Horrell... (n.d.). Retrieved from www.markhorrell.com/blog/2015/the-first-ascent-of-the-southwest-face-of-e

John Lewis: trouble in store - FT.com. (n.d.). Retrieved from www.ft.com/cms/s/2/92c95704-6c6d-11e5-8171-ba1968cf791a.html

Life Lessons from the Red Arrows - The Real Knightsbridge. (n.d.). Retrieved from http://therealknightsbridge.com/life-lessons-from-the-red-arrows/

British Road Cycling Team launches - Road Cycling UK. (n.d.). Retrieved from https://roadcyclinguk.com/news/racing-news/british-road-cycling-team-launches.ht

Tour de France: how Team Sky climbed to the top and stayed ... (n.d.). Retrieved from www.theguardian.com/sport/2013/jul/21/tour-de-france-team-sky-froome

Employee engagement updated research findings | Customer ... (n.d.). Retrieved from www.customer-insight.co.uk/article/808

How to Get Disengaged Employees to Go the Extra Mile ... (n.d.). Retrieved from www.americanexpress.com/us/small-business/openforum/articles/how-to-get-

3 Things That Separate Leaders From Managers | OPEN Forum. (n.d.). Retrieved from www.americanexpress.com/us/small-business/openforum/articles/3-things-th

Jack Welch - Alchetron, The Free Social Encyclopedia. (n.d.). Retrieved from http://alchetron.com/Jack-Welch-899165-W

Why Focus Is the Number-One Element of Business Success. (n.d.). Retrieved from www.entrepreneur.com/article/248563

Want to Be Successful? Focus on One Business. (n.d.). Retrieved from www.entrepreneur.com/article/244742

Think Different, Apple: Scrap The 'Special Events' | Fast ... (n.d.). Retrieved from www.fastcompany.com/3058152/apple-event/think-different-apple-scrap-the-s

Closing the Chasm Between Strategy and Execution - hbr.org. (n.d.). Retrieved from https://hbr.org/2013/08/closing-the-chasm-between-strategy-and-ex/

Modern Business Leadership: 4 Challenges and How to ... (n.d.). Retrieved from www.businessnewsdaily.com/6279-modern-leadership-challenges.html

What's the difference between leadership and management ... (n.d.). Retrieved from www.theguardian.com/careers/difference-between-leadership-management

What Makes a Leader? - Harvard Business Review. (n.d.). Retrieved from https://hbr.org/2004/01/what-makes-a-leader/ar/1

Four Theories of Leadership - Boundless Open Textbook. (n.d.). Retrieved from www.boundless.com/management/textbooks/boundless-management-textbook/lea

Transactional Leadership - Changing Minds. (n.d.). Retrieved from http://changingminds.org/disciplines/leadership/styles/transactional

About | Vince Lombardi. (n.d.). Retrieved from https://vincelombardi.com/about.html

Change Management - Essays - 23Sud - Free College Essays ... (n.d.). Retrieved from www.termpaperwarehouse.com/essay-on/Change-Management/104798

The Hard Side of Change Management - Harvard Business Review. (n.d.). Retrieved from https://hbr.org/2005/10/the-hard-side-of-change-management/ar/1

The Lego case study by John Ashcroft www.johnashcroftandcompany.com/

LEGO Case Study 2014. (n.d.). Retrieved from www.thelegocasestudy.com/uploads/1/9/9/5/19956653/lego_case_study_2014.pd

Tony Hsieh, Zappos, and the Art of Great Company Culture. (n.d.). Retrieved from https://blog.kissmetrics.com/zappos-art-of-culture/

Mikhail Gorbachev - The Last General Secretary of the ... (n.d.). Retrieved from http://history1900s.about.com/od/people/p/gorbachev.htm

10 Communication Secrets of Great Leaders - Forbes. (15 June 2017). Retrieved from www.forbes.com/sites/mikemyatt/2012/04/04/10-communication-secrets-of-great-leaders

Books

Collins, Jim - *From Good to Great*

Kim, W. Chan and Mauborgne, Renee - *Blue Ocean Strategy*

Yoffie, David and Kwak, Mary - *Judo Strategy*

Stalk, George and Lachenauer, Rob - *Hardball*

Sir Bonington, Chris - *Everest the Hard Way*

Cox, Peter - *Spedans Partnership - the story of John Lewis and Waitrose*

Kerr, James - *Legacy*

Peters, Steve - *The Chimp Paradox*

Welch, Jack - *Winning*

Ferguson, Sir Alex with Moritz, Michael - *Leading*

Lombardi Jnr, Vince - *What it takes to be #1*

Hsieh, Tony - *Delivering Happiness*

References

Websites

www.gottmaninstitute.com

www.physicsclassroom.com

www.jamesclear.com

www.harley-davidson.com

www.wardbyparker.com

www.ikea.com

www.roadcyclinguk.com

www.theguardian.com

www.customerinsight.co.uk

www.americanexpress.com

www.leadershipfactor.com

www.entrepreneur.com

www.fastcompany.com

www.harvardbusinessreview.org

www.businessdailynews.com

www.boundless.com

www.changingminds.org

www.vincelombardi.com

www.termpaperwarehouse.com

www.johnashcroft.com

www.legocasestudy,com

www.kissmetrics.com

www.about.com

www.forbes.com

www.ingramcontent.com/pod-product-compliance
Lightning Source LLC
Chambersburg PA
CBHW050528190326
41458CB00045B/6749/J